EMBRACEABLE YOU

We're All Part of the Story
New Hope, Pennsylvania

EMBRACEABLE YOU

We're All Part of the Story
New Hope, Pennsylvania

Edited by

Geri Delevich

and

Marilyn Cichowski

in association with Up River Productions, Inc.

iUniverse, Inc.
New York Bloomington

Embraceable You
We're All Part of the Story - New Hope, Pennsylvania

iUniverse books may be ordered through booksellers or by contacting:

iUniverse
1663 Liberty Drive
Bloomington, IN 47403
www.iuniverse.com
1-800-Authors (1-800-288-4677)

ISBN: 978-1-4401-7780-4 (pbk)
ISBN: 978-1-4401-7782-8 (cloth)
ISBN: 978-1-4401-7781-1 (ebk)

Printed in the United States of America

iUniverse rev. date: 10/23/2009

Editorial Team
Lynda Jeffrey Plott: developmental editor
Erika Jaeger-Smith: developmental editor
Patricia Lynch: copy editor

To people who embrace diversity, celebrate differences, and give new hope to all.

Table of Contents

Acknowledgments

When one takes on such an ambitious project, the number of people to thank could literally fill another volume. We thank every one of you. Everyone's generosity illustrates such an amazing sense of community and passion for this little borough of New Hope.

Thank you so much to all the writers who contributed. You are talented and loved.

Thanks to Lucianne DiLeo and Carolyn Ambler who helped on a daily basis. You are devoted friends.

Thanks to Joel Roberts and Rhea Rawley, your New Hope stories jump-started this project. You are inspiring.

Thanks to Erika Jaeger-Smith for your editing. You are knowledgeable.

Thanks to Patricia Lynch for your copyediting. You are efficient and gracious.

Thanks to Lynda Jeffrey Plott for your revisions, your timeliness, and your enthusiasm. You are an angel.

Thanks to Joseph Kelter of BadCat Design. Your patience and design skills are appreciated.

Thanks to Margie Perry. Your artwork and book cover are spectacular.

Thanks to our sisters, Mary Ann Albee and Lorraine Cichowski, for your continuous support. You are our cheerleaders.

Thanks to our Up River Productions, Inc. Board of Directors: Eric Albee, Bill Coda, George Kuebrich, and Art Mazzei. You are supportive.

Introduction

New Hope is a small, scenic river town nestled along the Delaware River in Bucks County, Pennsylvania. Located just hours away from Philadelphia, New York City, and most parts of New Jersey, it offers an enchanting escape from the fast-paced routines of daily life. Since the early 1900s, New Hope has attracted a following of artists from all walks of life. Painters, sculptors, writers, actors, and musicians have come to this picturesque place to soak up the beauty of the surrounding countryside and to enjoy the camaraderie of like-minded colleagues. Today, New Hope combines the historic charms and creative atmosphere of bygone days along with an edgy, eclectic, and playful style. "Quaint" and "Quirky" are two words I use often to describe this town. Yes, New Hope is still known as a haven for artists, but it is also . . . a paradise for shoppers, a showcase for antiques dealers, a hangout for food lovers, a romantic hideaway for couples, a fun-filled destination for families, a gathering place for entertainers, a hot spot for ghost hunters, a home for the famed Bucks County Playhouse, and a landmark village filled with numerous historic sites. Within just one square mile, New Hope offers you all of these amazing things.

I invite you to immerse yourself in the riches of our town. And what better way is there to get an intimate portrait of New Hope than by hearing from those people who know and love it best–the people who call it home. Home because they live here or home because part of this town now lives in them.

Within the pages of *Embraceable You*, fifty-four writers present their personal perspectives on New Hope. Many tell how they first arrived. All write about some aspect of why they love the New Hope area, whether it is the beautiful landscape, the history, the arts, the music, the food, the fun, or the wonderful people who have graced the streets of this town. Some of the writers are established authors, some are apprentice writers, and others enjoyed the process of collaboration as they wrote their stories with a little help from friends. The stories range from observances seen through the youthful eyes of an eight-year-old to the experiences of a ninety-four-year-old.

Each essay will give the reader a unique, colorful, and absorbing look at our town. Some writers are attracted to the history of the area, some reveal deeply personal remembrances of love and friendship, and others write about the way New Hope has served as a catalyst for their creative, emotional, and spiritual development.

You'll get a peek into the life of famous sculptor Selma Burke as told by one of her longtime New Hope friends. You will come to understand the impact noted woodworker George Nakashima had on a child who met him as a ten year old and then returned to the studio many years later to buy a piece of handcrafted Nakashima furniture. You'll discover how the tiny town of New Hope helped launch the career of United States Congressman Patrick Murphy. You will also discover that many famous personalities and historical notables such as Albert Einstein, George Washington, Abbie Hoffman, Julia Child, Norah Jones, Rod Stewart, Robert Redford, and Liza Minnelli had their moments in our town and, also, in our memories.

The authors of these stories comprise a wide range of individuals: residents, visitors, shop owners, town historians, community and spiritual leaders, entrepreneurs, past editors of the local newspaper, and renowned children's illustrator Dorothy Grider, as well as our elected officials State Senator Chuck McIlhinney and State Representative Bernie O'Neill. The ghosts of New Hope even check in with the help of writer Adi-Kent Thomas Jeffrey.

The New Hope cast of characters generously responded to the call to write their own personal stories. You'll enjoy the potpourri of writing styles and the variety of recollections. Each saga will help you to discover the magic and wonder of New Hope. Most of all, I hope you will come away with an understanding of how New Hope has energized and inspired people to feel, think, create, work, play, heal, and dream in countless ways.

As a teacher for thirty-three years, I've always believed we reach our maximum potential when we felt accepted and embraced by the people who surround us in our daily lives. This belief holds true within our families, our communities, and in our country. Perhaps the one quality that has made New Hope such an outstanding community throughout its history is the fact that it has always been a place where differences (whether they be racial, ethnic, religious, cultural, or sexual orientation) are not just tolerated–they are embraced and celebrated. William Penn founded Pennsylvania over three centuries ago based on the Quaker beliefs of equality, social justice, peaceful co-existence, and brotherly love. I think he would be proud to know that our town has become a shining example of a community committed to those same values. Through good times and bad times and the inevitable challenges that all communities face, we have been held together by a core conviction that all people should be respected for who they are as individuals. I believe it is this culture of openness, acceptance, and diversity that has allowed New Hope to prosper and thrive.

My vision of advancing the ideals of respect and unity resulted in the creation of Up River Productions, Inc. and the Embraceable You project. It is a three-fold endeavor that includes a documentary film, a music compact disc, and a book. The purpose of this entire project is quite simple: to demonstrate how our community exemplifies HOPE, not as a dream or an aspiration, but as a reality. It is my sincere wish that you, too, will find room in your heart to welcome and nurture this same spirit of inclusiveness and togetherness.

Once you embrace hope—anything is possible.

Geri Delevich

A Lasting Impression—
a Magical Moment with Jack Rosen

By Alan Fetterman

In the arena of culturally progressive communities, the Delaware Valley region is highly regarded, and the Delaware River is its meandering stream of strength. In turn, magnificent towns and communities have sprung up on both sides of the river, like cultural blossoms. The town of New Hope is one of them, a vibrant treasure trove brimming with history, cultural diversity, and artistic legacy.

As an insatiable artist, I have created art throughout the region including, of course, in New Hope. But as an artistic loner, I have always kept solitary and isolated in my journey. This changed one day when I was driving through New Hope and thought I saw the renowned photographer Jack Rosen, a magnificent American portrait photographer. I was unsure because we had never met.

The little I knew of Jack was that he was a deliberate, persistent, and committed man who passionately devoted himself to capturing the day-to-day life of human existence in a box of light, so he could present images for others to see and therefore feel. I knew that his work was highly acclaimed and appeared in many publications across the United States.

As I passed by the small café where he was sitting alone with his own thoughts, I became fairly certain that it was Jack Rosen. I drove on for a short distance, found a spot to park, walked back to say hello and express my admiration for his work—if it was Jack Rosen.

When I arrived at the café, I had no doubt. I put out my hand and said, "Hi. My name is Alan Fetterman. I wanted to tell you that I respect your work." He looked me dead in the eye, grinned, and squinted as though he snapped a picture with his eyes.

He replied brightly and abruptly, "I know your work, Alan Fetterman! As a matter of fact, I am looking at your shit right now. Oh don't worry, my work is shit and your work is shit because that's what an artist leaves behind."

At first, I was simply floored by the coincidence. What are the chances? There was Jack Rosen, a man I had never met, sitting quietly alone at a table on a side street looking at my work in a book, and I come by as though we had both arranged a meeting that day. Then I thought, "Wow! What a punchy guy to make such a bold and grotty statement about both his work and mine."

I quickly realized the honesty and directness of what he said and appreciated the fact that his thoughts were rich in spirit. I replied, "I like that." We talked a bit about his metaphor and then about how much dedication and commitment it takes to be an artist. We both agreed that it takes all of what one can deliver in order to be true.

After ten or fifteen minutes of conversation, I asked him if I could snap a photo of him sitting just where we met, to remember the moment. He said, "Yes, that's fine." I went to my Jeep, came back, and took the picture of Jack. I said, "Someday I would like to create a painting from the photograph on behalf of this magical moment." I asked if that would be all right with him. He nodded and said, "Yeah, sure. I like that." So the first and only time I met Jack Rosen was in New Hope, when he was sitting alone at an outside table of a little café looking through a book of my artwork. That experience was both serendipitous and magical. Many months went by while I pondered creating the painting about our chance meeting. Then one day, within a few hours the painting came out. I am not very methodical or premeditative as an artist. I am driven much more by fervor and need. When I complete a painting, I am always astonished because it comes out as such a surprise. For a few minutes, I pondered the fate of this painting and then I put it down.

After several days, I decided to put the painting up for sale and if by chance it sold, I thought it only fair to offer half the money to Jack. It seemed to me that we had been partners in all of this, and I wanted to divide the profits of the sale with him. I called him that day on May 17, 2006, in order to share my thoughts about the painting and what we would do. The phone rang. Someone answered, "Hello." I replied, "Hello, Jack." After a fleeting moment of silence, I heard the words, "No, this is his son Rick. Jack just passed away an hour ago."

In the end, the painting was a gift born from an artistic exchange and the ambient river of life's flow, as well as from the beloved town that the late Jack Rosen called home—New Hope, a vibrant treasure trove, brimming with history, cultural diversity, and artistic legacy.

Whistle-stop Town

By Heather A. Cevasco
In Loving Memory of My Father

When I was a very little girl (three- or four-years-old), I remember my father, Ed Cevasco, taking me with him when he went to work at the New Hope & Ivyland Railroad. At the time, I didn't know how much these weekend adventures with my dad would mean to me when I grew older. As a wide-eyed and curious toddler, I was captivated by the mystery and lore of those vintage trains. I loved to watch the fire of the coals burning. I would take a deep breath to smell the diesel, and nothing pleased me more than to hear the *long-short-long* sound of the train whistle blowing. Even today, many years later, the beautiful and haunting sound of a train whistle takes me back to my childhood days. In my mind's eye, I can still see my dad heading down those tracks.

Before I was born, my father enjoyed his twenty-eighth birthday celebration on board the train. Knowing that my dad had an absolute fascination with trains, my mother planned this trip as a surprise for him. After the round-trip excursion, my dad happened to strike up a conversation with some of the train workers who informed him that there was always a need for volunteers. Well that did it! Without skipping a beat, my father signed up as a volunteer. He joined the crew as a "fireman" shoveling the coal into the steam train. Eventually, he learned all the other skills necessary to run the steam train — good old Engine Number 40 and the diesel engines, too. It did not take long before my dad (the ultimate railroad enthusiast) had worked his way up to become the president of the New Hope Steam Railway.

I spent many of my weekends at the train yard, either working in the gift shop or helping to sell tickets. In those days, the railroad station was my favorite hangout. I loved being there and spending time with my dad. There was nothing he loved better than working at the station, running the locomotives, and chatting with the tourists. When my dad got married for the second time (to my stepmother), it wasn't in a church—no, it was on the train. We all stood at the front end of one of the diesel engines and watched them take their wedding vows. When they were pronounced "Husband and Wife," the train whistled like crazy!

New Hope has always been such an amazing town. As I grew up spending my weekends at the railroad station, I felt so at home and at ease. What an incredible place! In between train trips, I would walk around town popping in and out of my favorite stores such as the Now and Then shop and Love Saves the Day. Many of the shop owners knew me as "the girl from the train." I remember walking around town always feeling happy and safe. A place I frequented quite often was the small snack shop across the street from the railroad station. They had the best hot dogs around. It didn't take long for the weekend crew working on the trains to dub me their official "gofer." At the drop of a hat, I would make a quick run across the street to pick up dozens of hot dogs, chips, and ice cold sodas.

As I grew older, I got interested in acting, and I made my way from the railroad station to the Bucks County Playhouse. This theater has been a landmark in the Bucks County area for many decades. What a privilege it has been for me to work at the Playhouse alongside so many wonderfully talented individuals.

In looking back over the past years of my life, I honestly cannot count the number of times I hopped onboard one of those old New Hope & Ivyland locomotives. I also have no idea of how many acting roles I have assumed or how many stage productions I have attended at the Playhouse.

But I do know that I have countless memories of growing up in this wonderful town of New Hope.

"All Aboard!"

"Break a Leg!"

It doesn't get better than that.

What Exactly is New Hope?

By Janine Witte

A friend of ours once quipped that New Hope is the place where "the black sheep from all families come to stay." It is a haven for those who prefer to color outside the lines—for those whose motto is "live and let live." Residents embrace New Hope's eclectic mix of backgrounds, incomes, and lifestyles, whether they are proud descendents of New Hope's original families, recent transplants, or they wish to escape communities of conformity. We moved to New Hope in 1979. To my delight, I learned that our first house on Mechanic Street was once owned by my childhood hero, Jon Gnagy (the amiable, goateed host of the 1950s "Learn to Draw" TV program). The discovery of one of his art gum erasers hidden in a dark corner of a built-in cabinet was my proudest archeological find.

When we moved to North Main Street a year later, we learned that the canal-side cottage we just bought was once a "party house"—a gift from Mrs. Carson (who owned the riverfront house right across the street) to her husband. She had commissioned a former Frank Lloyd Wright student, Antonin Raymond, in the 1940s to design and build the tiny cottage on the wooded property adjacent to the towpath. Mr. Carson and Albert Einstein both worked in Princeton, New Jersey, and were good friends. As the story goes, Einstein used to stay overnight at the party house and play cards there with Mr. Carson and his other friends. We could only imagine the laughter, cigar smoke, and cold cuts sandwiches that entered the small, paneled rooms of this cottage on Friday nights!

Renowned portrait artist (and inventor of the character "Mr. Clean") Alden Wicks and his wife, Trippy, were the second owners of the cottage. They added another room to accommodate their family, and when they sold it to us, it was described as a house with a lot of "potential." However, it instantly felt like home to us. Over the years, we added more office, kitchen, and bedroom space, and crafted it into the contemporary home where we reside to this day. The creative spirit and inspiration of Einstein and Wicks remain, even though they would not even recognize the fully renovated "cottage."

In 1980, Paul and I were married on the back deck of our home—in a secret, spontaneous summer ceremony. Our wedding reception (attended by six people, including the minister and witnesses) was held in the rear garden of Mother's Restaurant, along with the other Friday night dinner customers. We laughed heartily, as our other friends found out one-by-one that we were just married. Some hid in the bushes while we dined and emerged later as their suspicions were confirmed. One person sent Angelo, "the singing telegram," to serenade us during our meal.

As relative newcomers to New Hope, with its inherent small-town charm and vibrant history, we were rapidly seduced by its collective energy and spirit. Art was (and still is) an integral component of New Hope's core appeal, and there were regular gallery shows, which became electrifying community social events. Occasionally, artists and other residents would face unforeseen personal or medical problems. Within weeks, New Hope would rally to sponsor a benefit, auction, or fundraiser in that person's honor. There were frequent public tributes to community activists who donated their time and services to New Hope's betterment. This was a caring, diverse and intellectually stimulating community. We were comfortable being part of it. We were home.

In the early 1980s, it was not unusual to see a Saturday morning parade on South Main Street—with a Borough Council member riding an elephant (an ironic sight in itself, since this Council member was a die-hard Democrat!) —and the beloved Grand Dame of the drag queens perched on the back of a convertible, doing her pageant wave while dressed as a flamboyant Martha Washington!

Mother's Restaurant was the gathering spot for weekend breakfasts and local chatter. Lines would form long before the doors opened at

9 AM, but there were plenty of distractions to make the time pass, whether it was conversing with fellow breakfast-goers, or salivating at the dessert and deli counter.

Spontaneous parties and gatherings abounded on the streets and in the neighborhoods. One weekend, we gathered on a friend's front stoop and formed a jug-and-washboard band—performing to the astonishment and delight of passersby. One curious pedestrian stopped, removed his trusty ukulele from its case, and joined in the fun! Congenial teens with unusual-colored hair, body piercing, and all-black attire sat and talked for hours on the Methodist church steps, generating astonished expressions from weekend tourists walking by. Artists, business owners, and other residents congregated at the sidewalk cafés and ice cream parlors—expressing opinions about politics and current events (two thousand residents with two thousand different opinions) or relaying humorous anecdotes. We used to joke that it would take forty-five minutes to walk the half mile from our house to the traffic light in town because there were so many friendly, talkative people all along the way.

As the 1990s emerged, New Hope became a poignant force in our lives. A local friend and microbiologist, Dr. Timothy Block, approached us with the story of a mutual friend whose child was diagnosed with chronic hepatitis B. We had never heard of the hepatitis B virus (HBV), and we questioned Tim's reasoning for approaching us specifically. Tim had just returned from a consultation with Oxford University professor and Nobel Laureate, Baruch Blumberg, who discovered the hepatitis B virus and was part of the team who developed the first HBV vaccine. With Dr. Blumberg's encouragement, Tim believed that we could help in some way, by starting a foundation devoted to creating awareness of HBV, with a primary objective of eventually discovering a cure for those who were chronically infected (hundreds of millions of victims worldwide).

Having since become accustomed to the idealism and spontaneity of New Hope happenings from the past, we did not flinch. Instead, we jumped right in and launched the Hepatitis B Foundation (HBF), along with Tim Block and his wife Joan. Paul designed the logo. We created flyers and literature, the first of which was our periodic newsletter, "B-Informed," under the direction of Jamie Fox. Interested New Hope residents attended our first organizational meeting, and our small ad hoc group chose me as its first president for a three-year term. With that came months of work, filing legal papers, registering as a tax-exempt organization, and acting as liaison with the IRS. Our new members became activists—writing letters, recruiting board members, and garnering support for our cause. Tim switched his focus from herpes research to HBV research and advocacy, and Joan emerged as a professional public speaker and the masterful editor of the HBF's award-winning, multilanguage website www.hepb.org. We could not have done this without the initial outpouring of support we received from the people of New Hope when the Foundation formed in February of 1991.

Our first fund-raiser was held at Luccaro's Restaurant (now Giuseppe's), and it was the most gratifying evidence of the value of New Hope's passionate response to our cause. We were able to enlist the help of U.S. Congressman Peter Kostmayer and State Senator Jim Greenwood, who both understood our case for creating awareness of the seriousness of HBV and spoke of the need to support our "Cause for a Cure." Most attendees had never heard of hepatitis B, but as our many guests gained understanding of the Foundation's critical mission, there was an overwhelming outpouring of support. As a result, we raised $17,000 that first night. We can proudly claim that New Hope put the Hepatitis B Foundation on the map, and it continues to be a renowned international research and outreach organization, attracting scientists from around the world.

Since its New Hope debut in 1991, the Hepatitis B Foundation, in partnership with Delaware Valley College, became co-owner of the building named the PA Biotechnology Center of Bucks County (in Doylestown)—which is home to the Foundation's offices and research labs, and hosts dozens of small biotech and start-up research companies. In its short history, the Hepatitis B Foundation has made important discoveries, extending and improving the lives of chronic HBV carriers.

New Hope became the "activist incubator" for many projects and endeavors since then—political, environmental, and social. People in this town immerse themselves in local causes—with a focus on the cause at hand and no expectations of reward, other than the satisfaction of contributing. Few communities can claim this degree of commitment. One of the most recent memorable fund-raisers held benefitted the Chamber of Commerce and New Hope Visitor's Center. It was called "Queen for a Day," a beauty contest comprising eight straight male contestants—each of whom were adopted, dressed, and coached by a drag queen or professional makeup artist from the area. Each contestant performed his own musical number (lip-synching) in full costume. Outfits ranged from the demure to the dangerous!

Paul was hesitant to participate at first, but as time and self-confidence progressed, he faithfully rehearsed his routine, and had a great time choosing his outfit with the aid of our friends Jim and Doug (affectionately known as our "wardrobe department"). Paul's coach and miracle-worker, Rick, transformed him into a beautiful auburn-haired bride, and he looked astonishingly youthful and radiant! All of the contestants performed to the delight and screams of the packed house—and the event was a huge success, exceeding its financial goals. Our town came through once again with this joy-filled celebration of diversity and community spirit.

When New Hope homes were submerged in the three major flood events between September 2004 and June 2006, the entire borough united to move residents' household items out of harm's way, dispense hugs and meals, help homeowners clean out basements, obtain supplies, and find temporary shelter. Twice we were the grateful recipients of that generosity of spirit and goodwill.

Our most recent joint community achievement was the launching of Patrick Murphy, our U.S. Congressman from the 8th District. In 2004, then Captain Murphy had just returned from a tour of duty with the 82nd Airborne in Iraq. Paul and I heard him give a speech during the John Kerry campaign, and he immediately impressed us with his sincerity, unwavering patriotism, and determination to make a difference. In 2005, Patrick contemplated a run for Congress for the upcoming 2006 election. Once again, New Hope spun its magic and got behind him—providing him temporary accommodations, his first campaign headquarters, political buttons, and local "meet-'n-greet" events. We believed in Patrick Murphy's work ethic and potential, and he, in turn, believed in the power of local grassroots organizing. He won by the narrowest of margins against a popular incumbent in 2006, but handily won reelection in 2008, and continues to recognize New Hope as the dawn of his political career.

So, what is it like to live here? The best way to express it is this: We don't live in New Hope nearly as much as New Hope lives in us, and will continue to live—no matter where our paths take us.

(Janine Witte and her husband Paul are thirty-year residents of New Hope.)

Visions of Our Past

By Will Rivinus

As you walk around New Hope today, let your historical imagination run wild. Look past the gift shops and tony restaurants on South Main Street to New Hope as it was one hundred years ago....

Look to the town when it was the busiest industrial center in Bucks County, when the Delaware Canal was the lifeblood of a manufacturing empire. Automobiles had been invented a few years earlier, but they were still a dangerous novelty along the Lower York Road, built to connect Philadelphia and New York. You could wait half a day to see two cars in a row. The covered bridge across the Delaware River charged a toll for horses and wagons going to Lambertville, New Jersey. The steam railroad line had just arrived from Ivyland and Philadelphia.

But, the canal...now that was transportation with a future. The canal brought anthracite coal down from the Pocono Mountains to fire the boilers of our factories and to make our kitchen stoves glow bright red. The canal brought lumber and stone from the upper Delaware, wheat and fresh vegetables from the farms, even a bit of raw whiskey from Bushkill, above Easton, Pennsylvania.

New Hope was blessed with an ideal location along the Delaware, one of the great rivers of eastern America. Racing through town toward the river, Ingham (Aquetong) Creek could bring upwards of sixteen million gallons of clear water from the fertile limestone valley to the west. The town was not in itself a farming community, but it enjoyed the bountiful harvests in one of the most productive areas in the nation.

When you entered New Hope on a canal boat, you were at the halfway point along the Delaware Canal thirty miles north to Easton where coal arrived via the Lehigh Canal; thirty miles south to Bristol where the canal boats enter the Delaware River at tidewater en route to Philadelphia. Just below town, there is an outlet lock where some boats crossed the river to enter New Jersey's Delaware and Raritan Canal en route to New York. However, no matter where you came from or where you were going, you had to pay tolls at New Hope's four locks that raised and lowered boats around Wells Falls in the river.

A century ago our mills were humming, long before bigger mills in Morrisville, Trenton, and Bristol overtook them. There were the older grain mills along Ingham Creek where farmers ground the wheat that had fed Washington's hungry troops a century earlier. Benjamin Parry had rebuilt the New Hope Mill in 1790 after a disastrous fire. That mill by the river gave our town its name. It would later house the Bucks County Playhouse.

A mile up Ingham Creek was the Heath Mill, circa 1702, one of the first gristmills in the county. Only a few stones remain on the ground to mark the site. Across Sugan Road was the Maris Mill, built in 1813 to process cotton from the South. Later this mill would be converted to handle silk, when American entrepreneurs thought they could beat the Chinese in that industry. Today that mill is a ruin, having endured a brief episode as a bed-and-breakfast inn.

Further upstream there was a large sawmill operated in the late nineteenth century by Samuel Ingham, who was, for a while, secretary of the Treasury under President Andrew Jackson. Such sawmills were common and were used for cutting virgin forests into board lumber for housing developments. The latest innovation in the lumbering business just before the Civil War was the prefabrication of standardized doors and windows that were shipped to city house sites by way of the canal.

There were two paper mills in town. The Union Mill was located along the Delaware River at the south end of town where the Waterworks condominiums now are. The other mill, located near the train station, was used to make shopping bags out of giant rolls of craft paper since 1888. Now that mill has been converted into upscale shops and offices called Union Square.

The prosperity of New Hope inspired all types of housing. There were mansions, elegant for their time. In the center of town on South

Main Street is the Parry Mansion, built in 1784, a handsome late Colonial home with outstanding local stonework. It stayed in the Parry family for more than a hundred years, until the New Hope Historical Society acquired and opened it for public visits.

Cintra, an elegant European-style home, was built by William Maris, across the road from the New Hope-Solebury High School. Maris built the house around 1824 when he was successful with the cotton mill nearby on Sugan Road. Unfortunately, he got into a legal wrangle with Benjamin Parry over control of the water flow driving mill wheels on Ingham Creek. He lost, so his house went to new owners, the most recent being an antiques dealer.

Yet another fine home is Springdale, the Huffnagle Mansion close to the Heath and Maris mills along Ingham Creek. Now a private home, this house boasts a ballroom and a backyard where exotic animals wandered. Sometime owner Charles Huffnagle had been the first United States Consul to Calcutta, India. When he returned to New Hope about 1850 he brought humped back cattle from India, an Arabian horse, Syrian goats, Chinese pigs, and other animals.

There were lots of average homes for the workers in New Hope, homes that you can admire along North Main Street today. Tucked back along Ferry and Mechanic Streets, and Old Mill Road were the boarding houses and modest row houses usually filled with immigrant Irish and English men and women recruited to work in the thriving mills. The town's economy has improved since then, but those converted buildings are easy to spot and unique in the farm country of Bucks County.

There were taverns, plenty of them, but they came and went with the times. The only mainstay is the Logan Inn adjacent to the canal and a block from the Bucks County Playhouse. There were churches, but religion has not fared so well over the years. The Methodist Church on South Main Street is now the restaurant Marsha Brown's. The tiny Presbyterian Church on West Ferry Street is now the town library. The Catholic congregation has moved to the outskirts of town, leaving its old church to become the expanded town hall.

On Sundays, the canal was a place for fun, when no canal boats were allowed to pass. Church groups would hold picnic excursions on the work scows. Small boys went swimming in the gentle current. Summer visitors, up for a week or two to cool off from sultry Philadelphia, were seen strolling arm-in-arm beneath giant sycamore trees. Early in the morning, a rowdy boatman might be seen staggering back to his tiny bunk in an idle canal boat. And as the sun reached its crest, you might spot a painter at an easel capturing the bucolic landscape on canvas. These were the settlers who would found the New Hope School of American Impressionism.

The canal boats that plied the Delaware Canal between 1832 and 1931 are gone, displaced by the railroad, the motorcar, and the public's preference for oil rather than coal. Where once there were as many as 3,000 canal boats, there is now only the occasional sightseeing tour boat in summer when the canal is full of water. Though the Delaware Canal is a State Park, a National Historic Landmark, and part of a National Heritage Corridor, it is not immune from the washouts caused by the floods of 2004, 2005, and 2006 that scoured the valley. Massive repairs are underway with federal funding and under the leadership of the Friends of the Delaware Canal. Someday soon, the canal will be rewatered and the mule bells will ring again along the towpath.

(Will Rivinus is a prolific author whose books include Guide to the Delaware Canal, *and* The Complete Guide to the Delaware and Lehigh National Heritage Corridor. *He has co-authored two books on the barns and farmhouses of Bucks County.)*

Nature's Peace

By McKenzie Rae

In the ever-changing landscape of New Hope, it is good to know I can count on something. Although its placid murky waters seem motionless, New Hope's canal is actually bursting with life. Just one step on the rusty-red towpath and you've escaped the suburban drone, or the hustle and bustle of tourists. The uplifting songs of birds at work, the gentle rays of sunshine, the cool breezes blowing off the Delaware, or my personal favorite—the charming houses dotted along the towpath, all add character to New Hope's wonderland of nature. The canal is an escape to a different world, a world that transcends time and the evolution that surrounds its banks. The canal's charm lies in its perfectly balanced ecosystem. The busy bees and beavers at work, the ducks and geese lazily grazing on its banks—all these creatures represent a perfect balance of work and play—from the animals to the people that journey on it.

The bicycle riders and runners whiz by making their marks on the dirt. Best friends and older couples stroll along sharing secrets and spreading love. The flowery fragrance of summer wildflowers mixed with the musty earthy odor lingers until autumn's crisp smells take over and with it, the trees form a canopy of amber and scarlet. The sparkle and twinkle of warm weather evolves into the peace of winter. The canal bears death so naturally and beautifully with glistening icicles and a white blanket that stretches as far as the horizon.

New Hope's proudest joy is Mother Nature's gift. The canal most importantly displays the harmony that can exist between man and nature. This man-made ditch has evolved into an endemic escape for

"New Hopeans" and visitors alike, and will be for many years to come. Whether it is winter, spring, summer, or fall, the canal proves timeless beauty and harmony are always "in" in New Hope, Pennsylvania.

Selma Burke—Rich in Friendship

By Paul Licitra

In a pocket full of change, I will instinctively look for a dime. That's my lucky coin. My dear friend, Selma Burke, was the artist who designed the portrait of Franklin Delano Roosevelt that graces our U.S. dime. Perhaps, you don't know much about Selma, so may I tell you a little bit about this remarkable woman?

Selma was the grand dame of African-American artists. She was born in the year 1900 to a farming family in North Carolina. From the riverbeds near her childhood home, young Selma delighted in the discovery of transforming squeezed clay into molded objects. Right then and there, a young artist was born.

Selma pursued her artistic career with great determination. She became involved in the Harlem Renaissance movement and served as a sculptor's model. In the late 1930s, she won a grant that helped her to travel to Europe. She studied ceramics in Vienna and then went on to Paris to study with Aristide Maillol, the neoclassical sculptor. Selma also took private art lessons from Henri Matisse who became her mentor. After earning her doctorate degree in sculpture from Columbia University, Selma worked happily and tirelessly at her craft. Every spare moment found her chiseling away with a chunk of brass, stone, or wood in her hands.

In 1943, she won a nationwide competition to create a portrait of F.D.R. Her bronze plaque served as the model for the relief profile of the President that appears on the dime. Needless to say, this sealed her reputation as an artist. I think it's interesting to note that President Roosevelt sat for Selma seven times. When Selma showed her final rendition to the president's wife for approval, she vividly recalled Eleanor Roosevelt's criticism. "You have made him look too young." Selma replied, "I have not made him for today, but for tomorrow and tomorrow. Five hundred years from now America and the entire world will want to look on our president, not as he was the last few months before he died, but as we saw him for most of the time he was with us—strong, so full of life, and with that wonderful look of going forward." Selma was a true visionary.

Throughout her lifetime, Selma faced one marital challenge after another. When she was twenty-eight-years old, she married Durant Woodward who had been a close childhood friend of hers. She was widowed a year later. During her years in New York, she was introduced to the African-American poet and writer, Claude McKay, who was a major figure in the Harlem Renaissance. They had a tumultuous relationship—she married and divorced him twice. In 1949, Selma married again, this time to Herman Kobbe, a famous architect. The couple moved from New York to New Hope. They bought a beautiful estate outside of town in Solebury where Selma had a studio built on the property. Together the two of them initiated an active role as members of the New Hope art community. Tragically, Herman died in 1955.

After she was widowed, work became Selma's main outlet for solace. She was perpetually busy in her New Hope workshop creating new pieces. Her themes ranged from classical to contemporary. She was most well known for her historical figures: Duke Ellington, Booker T. Washington, John Brown, and Calvin Coolidge. At the age of eighty, Selma produced her last monumental work—an eight-foot sculpture of Dr. Martin Luther King, Jr., that stands in Marshall Park, North Carolina.

Although known primarily for her sculptures, Selma was a multitalented artist. She loved to paint and was equally versatile in using watercolor, oil, and acrylics. Selma was truly a pioneer in the world of visual arts. Not only did she create impressive works of art exhibited in countless museums around the world, she was also an influential and gifted teacher. She taught, she lectured, and she tutored other artists. For years, she held an appointment to the Pennsylvania Council on the Arts. She founded two art schools—one in Pittsburgh and the other in Harlem, New York. Most of all, Selma was a tireless advocate, and a dynamic role model for other aspiring African-American artists in America. I am hopeful that this brief description of Selma's accomplishments has given you a glimpse of what a powerful and inspirational woman she was as an international public figure.

Now, I want to tell you about Selma, my friend. From the moment I first met Selma, I absolutely loved her. The year was 1978, and I was serving on the committee for the annual Bucks County Sculpture Exhibition. It was Selma, who spearheaded the exhibition, which I might add, continues to this day. The show would be devoted exclusively to three-dimensional art. It was the first of its kind held in Bucks County. In an effort to promote this first, small exposition, Selma generously donated one of her own sculptures as an item that would be raffled off at the show. I was hired as the caterer of the event. I designed the menu and took great pleasure in preparing the food. Although I was busy in the kitchen, I took the time to buy five dollars worth of raffle tickets. And guess what? I won! I left that night with a new companion—an alabaster lady who perpetually sits in a position of "Repose." She is thick, and bold, and sensuous. As she sits, her knees are pulled up to her forehead. Her head rests on her knees. I love her. I wish I could say that she is one of a kind, but Selma had another idea! With my permission, we took the alabaster piece to an atelier in Philadelphia who used it to make a mold. Working with metal, he reproduced two more ladies in "Repose." My noble Italian alabaster figurine ended up with a set of heavyweight bronze twin sisters!

Eventually, my catering business expanded into a full-fledged restaurant business. In 1979, I bought the Towpath Restaurant on Mechanic Street in New Hope. Selma was a regular at the restaurant. She would come often, and it would not be unusual for her to stop by with a host of other local artists. Selma had a magnetic personality and such a grand manner. She was fun and jovial. People were naturally drawn to her. And, oh, how she loved to tell stories! Selma could regale a group for hours telling stories about her own life. She was charming, captivating, and entertaining. She was the center of attention—there was no one else like her. As I watched her sitting at one of the tables in my restaurant, surrounded by friends and admirers, I would remind myself that many years ago (when Henrietta Cunningham owned the Towpath House) Selma was a real "trailblazer," for she was the first

African-American person who ever came through the doors of this dining establishment. Now, here she was holding court in the Towpath Restaurant. I thought to myself, "You go, girl!"

Selma was a brilliant woman, and it should come as no surprise, that she was also quite competitive. At the age of seventy, she completed her second doctorate degree in arts and letters from Livingston College in North Carolina. Selma also held eight honorary doctorate degrees for her lifelong efforts and contributions. In 1979, President Jimmy Carter presented her with the honorary award "Outstanding Achievement in Visual Arts." In 1987, she was the recipient of the Pearl S. Buck Foundation Award for her professional distinction and her devotion to humanity. Selma received numerous other awards and accolades, along with international acclaim, but in spite of all these honors, she used to say to me, "Paul, I'm not there yet. I want to have as many doctorate degrees as Marion Anderson!" I used to chuckle to myself because Selma was always trying to top her.

Selma and I remained devoted friends for many years. Our connection was so strong. Selma and I traveled together to Mooresville, North Carolina, when her hometown was holding a celebration to honor her artistry and vision. I also took a trip to Charlotte, North Carolina, to see the towering, full-length figure sculpture she created of Martin Luther King, Jr. This was Selma's last monumental work. It is an awe-inspiring depiction of the civil rights leader. The eight-foot figure of this great man is shown walking up steps with his right arm upraised. Selma inscribed the sculpture with these words, "Dr. Martin Luther King, Jr. who dared to make the American dream of freedom for all Americans a reality."

Selma herself never stopped dreaming her own dreams. Even in the face of adversity (for years, Selma suffered from physical complications because of diabetes and in the last months of her life she was battling cancer) she still continued to work. At ninety-three, Selma had accepted a federal commission to sculpt Rosa Parks—a project she was working on right up until her death.

Selma trusted me as her closest confidant and friend. I was the one who was there with her as she went through many difficult days. When the doctors wanted to amputate her leg because of gangrene in the knee, she defiantly told them, "No." I stayed with Selma and nursed her back to health. I am happy to say that with her determination and my constant care and encouragement, Selma got back up on her feet again.

Selma died on Tuesday, August 29, 1995. She was ninety-four years old. A community tribute to her took place at Green Hills Farm, the Pearl Buck estate. This was such an appropriate setting for a memorial service since Selma had enormous admiration for Pearl Buck. In the gardens of the estate, there is a beautiful statue of Pearl Buck entitled "Uplift" which is one of Selma's creations.

Following the service, I knew I had an important job to do. Selma had entrusted me with her last wishes. She wanted to be cremated and she asked that her ashes be scattered in the Delaware River. Fortunately, I had a friend whose house was located right along the river. In addition, the house had a floating dock. I carried the urn of ashes, and accompanied by a small group of friends, I proceeded out to the end of the dock. As I was kneeling down, sprinkling her ashes into the water—WHOOSH . . . a huge wave swept over me! "That's okay," I thought to myself, "I'm going to finish what I set out to do." I continued to distribute her ashes and finally when I was done, I got up—only to discover that I was dry as a bone!

Some things in life are beyond explanation, but I like to think it was Selma's incredibly strong life force that caused the big wave to sweep over me. To me, it was a final "wave" good-bye, as well as a great big, "thank you!" And, since Selma always seemed to sweep through life with so much magic in her heart and soul, I'm not surprised that she left me standing there a bit bewildered . . . "Hmmm, I wonder why I'm not soaking wet after that experience? Oh well, I'll just chalk it up as one last reminder of Selma's dry sense of humor!"

Selma Burke left her mark on the U.S. dime . . . and she also left her imprint on me forever. Will you do me a favor? Reach into your pocket, find a dime, and think of Selma. I always do.

(Paul Licitra has lived in the New Hope area for more than thirty years. He is the owner of Tuscany on the Towpath Restaurant on Mechanic Street, New Hope. Paul has a longtime involvement in theater and the arts.)

Covering New Hope Becomes a Deeper Pursuit

By Scott Edwards

I arrived in New Hope, Pennsylvania, in 2002, at the age of twenty-five. Having grown up in Langhorne, about twenty minutes away, I had visited New Hope many times before. But my visit was of a more permanent nature this time. I had been promoted to be editor of the *New Hope Gazette*, a weekly community newspaper in existence for about fifty years. I had spent the previous four years working for the InterCounty Newspaper Group, which comprises the *Gazette* and five other weeklies in and around Bucks County. However, my news writing experience was limited. I helped develop, launch, and then produce the Group's arts and entertainment publication in the year prior to taking the editor job. The arts and entertainment were where my professional and personal interests lay, which made the *Gazette* an appealing opportunity. It was an atypical newspaper, at least for our group, because it reflected a community whose news almost entirely stemmed from the arts. I accepted the position because it was a big step forward in my career. I, of course, had no idea at the time the sort of impact it would have on my life as a whole.

Home is where the office is

Sometime during the eighty-hour workweeks and the constant barrage of criticism that formed my first year at the *Gazette*—at least that's what I remember foremost—New Hope became my home—first figuratively and then literally. I was living in the trendy Old City section of Philadelphia when I began working in New Hope. But, gradually, I was spending more time in New Hope, in part because of work and, too, because I'd met a girl—miraculously, given how little free time, let alone a personal life, I had at that time—who lived and worked in New Hope.

The complaint registered most often during the early days at the paper, both by my bosses and the *Gazette* readers, was that I was covering the wrong things. I had no idea what this meant. Everything that I was filling the pages of each issue with was New Hope–related as far as I could tell. Making matters worse, as frequently as the complaint was served, it never grew more specific. The longer and harder I worked, the more I felt as though I was stumbling through a pitch-black room searching for a doorknob. In retrospect, it makes sense when and why things began to click. I was, all along, attending almost all of the ribbon-cuttings, the meet-and-greets, and the press conferences myself, playing dual roles each time as reporter and ambassador.

New Hope is a borough of a square mile, and I felt like I was personally lifting every rock, shaking every hand. However, I wasn't shaking *every* hand. It was not until I began living in New Hope that I started to comprehend what exactly I was missing. I didn't actually move to New Hope until almost three years after I took the *Gazette* job. But for all intents and purposes, I was living there long before then because of my relationship.

Where I saw a very distinct New Hope form before me through my editor's eye, a completely separate one took shape once I began to move about it as one of its members, to dine and drink here, to develop friendships here. Soon, I bridged the gap between the two worlds until they became one and the same. The complaints—well, at least that one complaint—stopped. When the relationship ended, I returned to Philadelphia during my nights and weekends, but it became quickly apparent where I felt most at home. Since my freshman year of college, I have called several places home, but New Hope was the first actually to feel like one. Meeting friends for drinks at The Raven, walking out on the Delaware River wing dam on a clear summer night, eating mashed potato pizza in The Swan courtyard, debating political stances across a

Village 2 kitchen counter—these were the images that seeped into my subconscious and now defined my idea of home.

A made-for-TV movie plot

The ironic twist is that once I moved to New Hope, in early 2005, I began to bypass the social scene more often than I indulged in it. I blame the aging process. A good, severe hangover required almost a week of recovery by that point. Accepting the occasional dinner party invitation seemed to satisfy and exhaust my quota. As I turned away from the bars along Main Street, yet another side of New Hope and the surrounding region began to present itself. I started riding a bike for the fun of it and then for the sport of it and then out of pure addiction. I began on the towpath, but I transitioned to the road when I sought more challenging terrain and longer routes. I would ride until sunset after work on weekdays. And on weekends, I'd ride for several hours at a time. Something in the suffering spoke to me on a level in which I had never before communicated.

Even more important than the testing of physical limits for me was the exploration of my new home, an experience that made my heart rate jump as easily each time out as a steep climb. The architecture, the landscape, the isolation—all of it jived perfectly with the direction I was determined to take my life, both in that precise moment on the bike and in the much larger sense, away from it. Not a day has passed in the four-plus years that I have made my home in New Hope, where I don't pause to consider for even a fleeting moment how fortunate I am to be here. Usually it's for a different reason each time.

As fate would have it—or at least most made-for-TV movie writers—I discovered the love of my life here—right next door, actually. And while we're both hungry to embrace the unknown, to see the world, and experience exotic things and settle down and make a life together for ourselves, I know it will all be easier and more meaningful to do now because we have such a solid point of reference. We know what home feels like. Moreover, we know that we can always come back to it—if, that is, we ever drift from it in the first place.

Townie

By Joel E. Roberts

I moved to New Hope in 2000 because I found what might have been the last available bargain for a building in town and because my best friend told me to. I believe I may have driven through town once before in my life because I do, sort of, remember the river drive.

For five years after my divorce, I lived in a small Cape Cod community where I found the summer life easy, but the winter life full of drunks, which meant little business and lonely weeks in a very quiet New England town. If you are okay with that, then please forgive me, and my feelings, about it, but I just had to get out of there—before I became one of them.

I found what might have been the last remaining "dump" in New Hope though it still took way too much money to turn it into a place where I could both easily live and work. It took two long years to rehabilitate my home on Mechanic Street, but it took about five minutes for me to adjust to my new life.

Living in the downtown section takes what I have come to realize is a very special person—and some serious home insulation. If you choose to live in town you have to also live with those who come to town, those who party in town, and those who walk around town at all hours of the evening and early morning. I have gone to bed with people sitting on my front bench laughing and talking at two o'clock in the morning and have awakened to the sound of a man standing in the middle of my street talking to no particular listener.

I keep thinking I have met almost everyone in town and then someone else pops up and surprises me. The first people I met here were Joe and Tom. They were Mechanic Street icons in their day and claim to have operated a store in every building on the street at one time. I asked Joe, who was in his late eighties, if he was ever in the military and he answered that he sure was—he spent the war as the concierge on the Queen Mary. They had what I claim is the "New Hope Sense of Humor." They could talk your ear off with stories of New Hope's notorious past as well as what was going on in almost everyone's bedroom in town.

It was in 2000 that I moved to town and in the last nine years a lot of things have changed here. I tell people who come into my store complaining that so-and-so's store has closed and moved away or that the town sure has changed since earlier days, that what they never realize is that New Hope changes every five minutes. Every time you turn around new people are coming to town…buying places…renting stores…tearing down the old and seemingly useless, and building what they believe to be their own dream.

New Hope is a town full of people creating and living their dreams. It is a town where if you were paddling your canoe lazily down the Delaware River some night you would hear the sound of the place a mile away. The town has a specific sound, a thump, so-to-speak, and it sparkles even during a flood with everyone's energy. We're the weirdest bunch of folk most people have met and every one of us shines that badge with a special polish. Come and sit in on a town meeting sometime to see what I mean.

Everyone just seems to get along, and it is the only place I've ever been where the people who work here seem to love what they do, whatever it may be. New Hope to me is a very special place. Basically, it's a grand old rivertown along the Delaware with a "weirdo" problem you have to see to believe.

A Tribute to Mother (Joe) Cavellucci

By Marilyn Bullock

Why do I love New Hope? Why do I own and run a website called ILoveNewHope.com? Because, like so many before me and those yet to come, I fell in love with the lush history and extraordinary energy of this town, with the fascinating people who live and work here, and with the magnitude and range of creative endeavors based here. It has become my HOME.

In 2000, I partnered with Keith David, then co-owner of the Mansion Inn, on the website NewHopePennsylvania.com (now ILoveNewHope.com.) Below is the very first article I wrote for the Faces & Places section of ILoveNewHope.com. It is based on a true story told to me by my next-door neighbor, Scott. In addition, I have quoted Robert Ebert, himself a New Hope icon, who was, at the time, the owner of the Raven Inn and Restaurant.

One evening a handsome young man of nineteen ventured into the bar of the Raven for the first time. In search of a quiet glass of wine and perhaps some innocent conversation, he settled in for several minutes before noticing that an older "woman" was staring at him. She gave him a slight wink, slowly and deliberately opened her purse, took out a scarlet lipstick, and deftly painted her lips. After chicly blotting her lips with a tissue, she gently folded the tissue and then, much to the young man's surprise, passed it over to him.

A scene from "La Cage aux Folles"?

Perhaps.

But this scene took place in New Hope in the mid–1970s and starred the beloved local gay celebrity, "Mother." Mother was known for many things, none of which was subtlety.

Mother, born Joe Cavellucci in the early 1920s, was a fixture in New Hope for over forty years. Joe was a "character out of Charactersville," laughed Robert Ebert, owner of the Raven Inn and Restaurant, where Mother once worked as a waitress. When asked what made Mother so notable, Robert said, ". . . because he was such a visibly gay person, long before it was acceptable to be gay—even in New Hope. He walked with aplomb through all crowds."

Joe's life was full of contradictions. He lived as a she for most of his life; he was devoutly religious and a great joke-teller; he was outrageous and caustic, yet loving and generous. People from all walks of life called Joe "Mother," "Mom," or even "Mommy." Over the years, he acquired many "children." Mother was primarily known for walking everywhere—since he didn't own a car—in his tight skirts, stiletto heels, bouffant hairdos (his own hair!), and the ever-present purse.

Sadly, Mother left us in May of 2000. Cancer may have taken the body, but her spirit will enchant New Hope forever. Perhaps we'll catch glimpses of her yet, another of New Hope's "ghosts," strutting through town to the distant whispers of days long gone.

The Original Ghost Buster

By Lynda Jeffrey Plott

Adi-Kent Thomas Jeffrey, Bucks County's original ghost chaser was my mother! She was a bright, beautiful, and fearless woman, filled with *joie de vivre* and a bold sense of adventure.

My mother spent over forty years researching and writing about supernatural phenomena that occurred all over the world, but she always returned to her beloved Bucks County because she believed that no place on earth was more abundant with haunted spirits than the Delaware Valley area. She concluded that New Hope, in particular, held more ghosts and specters per square mile than any other place on earth.

Adi-Kent Thomas Jeffrey was a brilliant researcher, and a probing reporter. She set out each day with her notebook in hand to explore and to document the eerie happenings in the Delaware Valley area. The result of her investigations led her to compile the true tales that she had gathered into an anthology of ghost stories. Her two books, *Ghosts in the Valley*, and *More Ghosts in the Valley*, published in the early 1970s, presented her readers with authentic accounts of haunts and spirits that lurked along the dark side of the Delaware.

The ongoing popularity of these books led my mother into another successful business venture. In 1982, she founded the company Ghost Tours of New Hope. Swinging her candle-lit lantern, and looking like the New York fashion model that she once was, my mother would lead people from one haunted site to another. Her chilling accounts of genuine spooks and supernatural spirits put New Hope on the map as a desired destination for ghost seekers.

Mother's dear friend, Adele Gamble, took over the ghost tour business in 1986, when my parents moved to Washington, D.C. Adele's hard work, steadfast dedication, and bubbling enthusiasm have contributed to many years of continued success for Ghost Tours.

My mother spent a lifetime chasing ghosts and never stopped until she went to join them. I am sure that her vibrant spirit still floats and glides and dances over New Hope...the place she dubbed the most charming, and the most haunted village in this entire world.

I hope you will enjoy the following excerpt, taken from her classic series of ghost books, which illustrate the mysterious and compelling atmosphere of New Hope. *HAPPY HAUNTING!*

(Lynda Jeffrey Plott, a current resident of Washington D.C., inherited from her mother a love for the written word as well as a reverence for the unknown mysteries of this world.)

[Excerpt taken from the book, *Ghosts in the Valley,* by Adi-Kent Thomas Jeffrey.]

"The Inn-Place for Haunters"

When Carl Lutz bought the old Logan Inn in New Hope (in the late 1960s), he found he owned not just an historical building, but a legend. Not long after that, he discovered he housed a score of inexplicable phenomena as well.

The Logan Inn was originally the local tavern of Coryell's Ferry, the main crossing of the Delaware River above Trenton before, during, and after the Revolution. Located on the much-used stagecoach route between Philadelphia and New York, the hostelry was a popular place. It was called in those days simply, "The Ferry Tavern."

The inn was heavily frequented during the War of Independence and must have throbbed to the rafters when General George Washington's men were quartered there and made wassail that Christmastime of 1776, drinking to the success of their cause and the downfall of King George the Third in his American colonies.

After the war years, the inn continued to be the focal point in the life of the townspeople for they gathered there to quaff ale and exchange news of the day. One time around 1790 this news was high disaster for the village—a whole complex of mills located there burned to the ground.

As the town recouped from the loss and the mills were rebuilt, the village changed its name from "Coryell's Ferry" to "New Hope"... the name it bears to this day.

The inn, however, retained its same name well into the nineteenth century. Then in 1829, its owner, a Mr. Steele, sold it to the village's oldest resident, Abraham D. Meyers. The incoming landlord gave his tavern a new name indigenous to the area—the name of Logan. He called it, "The Logan House."

The historical background that intrigued Mr. Meyers was the incident in which William Penn's secretary, James Logan, wishing to express his brotherhood with the Indians, exchanged names with the Lenni Lenape chief. He took the Indian's name for his own and gave his illustrious "James Logan" to the chieftain.

In commemoration of this friendly act and as a unique hallmark, so to speak, for the inn, Meyers commissioned a local craftsman, Samuel Cooper, to create a large weathervane in the form of the Indian Logan. Cooper worked it out of sheet metal and mounted the image on a forty-foot pole in front of the tavern.

All went well for the great chieftain for more than a hundred years. Then one night in the mid-years of this century the pole suddenly broke and the inn's owner stashed it away in the barn at the rear of the property.

That night (and it was February 22, the anniversary of the birth of Mr. Coryell's great Revolutionary friend, George Washington) a fire broke out in the barn and nearly everything was destroyed. On that night also was born the legend that if one moved the Indian from his accustomed place, fire would break out! The durable chieftain then was placed on a post a few feet tall in front of the inn once more, the post being considered a reasonable substitute for the old pole.

Carl Lutz, though, did not consider it a fair exchange. He decided the metal figure should rest imposingly on a forty-foot pole as it originally did. Cautiously, he ordered the sign reinstated on a tall pole overlooking the inn's lawn. As the order was carried out, he noticed it was February 22, 1971!

"I was not cowed by that realization," says Carl Lutz. "I was putting him back where he belonged. I knew he could only be pleased by that."

"As if to confirm Logan's pleasure with this act," notes Carl with amusement and satisfaction, "it rained on Washington's birthday and for five consecutive days afterwards. Assurance for us that there would be no fire!"

"The inn is filled with strange phenomena and a host of ghostly doings," Carl concludes. "I could go on and on. But we all agree that the spirits who haunt this place are friendly and want to look after us. As long as I'm here, they'll always be welcome."

And with a wink he adds, "I believe that Chief Logan himself is smiling down on us from his happy haunting ground!"

No doubt, a trail of mystery will always surround this beloved old inn.

[Excerpt from the upcoming book, *A Gathering of Ghosts,* by Adi-Kent Thomas Jeffrey. To be published posthumously in 2009. Last in the series of Mrs. Jeffrey's ghost books.]

"Curtain Call"

Coming to New Hope along South River Road you will soon find yourself approaching the famous Bucks County Playhouse built from the old Parry gristmill. Its walls and floorboards have reverberated to the voices and footsteps of hundreds of luminaries. Everyone knows that, but what few people know is that these walls have encased some unearthly doings.

For one thing, the costume-changing area below, over by the dam, is the habitat of spirits from the past. Several people who are closely associated with the Playhouse feel that. Many of them have told me there is definitely a feeling of a presence down in that old area, which is part of the original gristmill.

Not so long ago, the musical director there at the time, Newton Gilchrist, told me the same thing. "There is unquestionably a presence down in that old storage area. I have felt it many times." Most unsettling of all though, to the entire cast of one performance, was the eerie experience that happened a few years ago (1979) when the group was putting on the show *Music Man.* Newton was in the musical himself and still vividly remembers the incident. "The entire cast was on stage," he recalled to me, "and it was a moment of action. No one was singing at the time when suddenly a strong, high-pitched voice shrilled out in front of the theater. We were rocked." The producer hastily rushed upstairs thinking the sound box was on and that someone was up there singing away. He was stunned to find the room completely empty. Now, could it have been a call from beyond while everyone was on stage? Did any traumatic event occur in connection with the Playhouse in the past that could have caused such a disturbing interruption? A voice from an unhappy situation that had once occurred?

I found that there had been one.

When the *Lion in Winter* was playing in New Hope with George C. Scott in 1966, the role of Philip, King of France, was played by a handsome young actor who persistently came on stage stoned out of his mind. Although he was warned by his fellow actors and the director and everyone else, he seemed unable to heed their advice. He was always coming on stage and interrupting the other actors with some kind of slurring dialogue or muttering. One time during a performance, he did this to Scott. After the show, George C. seized the youth by his collar and yelled, "You S.O.B.! If you ever do that to me on stage again, I'll kill you!"

The actor, obviously a disturbed young man, went back to New York a few months later, poured kerosene over himself, and lit a match. He did not die. He was rescued before complete destruction, but the results were dire nevertheless. He lost both ears and his lips, and would never again stride across the stage as a handsome hero. After that, he played only minor character parts.

So the question remains . . . Did he return with revengeful thoughts that summer evening in 1979 to the place that continued to haunt his memory? One final interruption by a self-destructive actor still burning with anger for vindication?

Embrace the Mystery

By Adele Gamble

I followed in her footsteps up and down Mechanic Street, along the towpath, past the Parry Mansion, spellbound by the strange and unusual tales this woman was recounting. The crowd following this well-known "Ghost Lady" consisted of the just plain curious, the fun-seekers, the skeptics, and a few like me who were the true believers. I was immediately enchanted by the mystery and the intrigue of these strange happenings which Adi-Kent Thomas Jeffrey considered not just legends, but true ghost stories.

In fact, Adi had written two best-selling books documenting the history of many unsolved mysteries and haunted happenings in and around the Delaware Valley area. The ghost tour business Adi started in 1982 was founded on her desire to make New Hope a prime destination for all ghost hunters, as well as to bring a little enchantment and entertainment to the village.

Once was not enough, I wanted more. So I came back and took a ghost tour for a second time. Just as I expected, I was enthralled once again by these spine-chilling stories. Even more than that, I felt a strong bond and kinship with Adi. We talked. We exchanged ideas. We shared stories. It was an immediate connection. We just "clicked." It wasn't long before Adi pointed a finger in my direction, and said to me in no uncertain terms, "You are going to be a Ghost Tour guide. I want you!" Adi's sixth sense never steered her wrong. She knew we both had an affinity for the supernatural.

For four years, we worked together side by side. We designed ghost tours with a special twist: "Ghosts 'n Gifts," "Dinner with a Ghost,"

35

"Spirits of Christmas Past," "Night in a Haunted House," and "Haunted Village Weekend: A Bewitching Retreat into the Beyond." In the spring, we marched as "Ghosts Come Back to Life" in the New Hope Flower Festival Parade. In the autumn, Adi hosted a Ghost Dinner Theater show at Paul Licitra's Towpath House. I transformed myself from a Ghost Tour guide into a Ghost Tour Drama Queen! "The minute I laid eyes on you, dear, I just knew you had to be the 'Ghost in Green Silk'," Adi said. As she helped me into my long, flowing, green taffeta costume and handed me the pewter cup filled with fake arsenic, I knew I was ready to make my acting debut. I ironed a ghostly countenance onto my face, fixed my gaze to the world beyond, and then floated past the audience to the lilting sounds of a lute player. The show was a smashing success.

Adi and I were a dynamic duo. We shared a close friendship for many years. In 1986, the time seemed right finally for Adi to say good-bye to her beloved Bucks County. She was headed to Washington, D.C., so that she could live close to her daughter. I became the new owner and manager of the Ghost Tours business. The torch had been passed from the "Mistress of the Macabre" to the "Ghost in Green Silk."

Ghost Tours of New Hope has now been in operation for close to three decades. During my twenty-three years as director, I have never lost my passion and enthusiasm for the invisible beings that surround and encompass this village. As visible proof of this love, I even had a ghost tattooed on my ankle. Not many people are a walking advertisement for their business, but I am. With a lot of hard work and perseverance, the business has continued to thrive, grow, and evolve. Ghosts are never static, you know! It is clear to me that New Hope is definitely a top-notch area on the goose bump scale. Over the years I have collected so many new stories from both the past and the present, and that is what makes my work so alluring and exciting. You never know when or where a ghost might decide to enchant you, inform you, or try to scare you.

During the year of our twenty-fifth anniversary celebration, Scott Randolph produced a documentary film entitled *Ghost Tours of New Hope*. As I sat in the audience watching the premier showing at the Bucks County Playhouse, I was absolutely thrilled to see some of my favorite ghost stories brought to life. For years, I have told the riveting tale of the hitchhiker, a young man with bright yellow hair and piercing blue eyes who appears and reappears all along the dark highways of this area. In the film, you will see a wonderful reenactment of this ghostly traveler who causes two brash and self-assured teens to finally lose their cool. Like many others, I have always found that suspense is the best entertainment of all.

In looking back over the years, I will always remember the day I took my first Ghost Tour around New Hope. Without realizing it, I was being drawn into a place and a world where time stands still. Destiny found me…and I've been following in her footsteps ever since.

(Adele Gamble is the owner and manager of Ghost Tours of New Hope.)

Love at First Sight—
Thanks, Abbie Hoffman

By Norma Quarles

In the spring of 1983, while working as a reporter for NBC News in New York City, I was given the assignment of covering a protest in Bucks County, Pennsylvania. A large protest was being waged to stop a proposed pumping station from being built in Point Pleasant. The pump would divert the Delaware River forty miles inland to the Limerick Nuclear Power Plant. Leading the protest was the controversial and infamous Abbie Hoffman. Hoffman, an antiwar protestor from the Vietnam era, had been a fugitive. For quite a while he lived underground with a new identity, but finally he decided to give himself up. He served half of a three-year sentence before being paroled. Hoffman was a committed environmentalist and successfully fought to protect the St. Lawrence River from winter navigation before heading to Bucks County in hopes of protecting the Delaware River.

I arrived the night before the Point Pleasant rally and stayed at the Holiday Inn in New Hope. I left early the next morning ... about 6:30 AM, and headed north to Point Pleasant. As I drove up Route 32 with the sun glistening on the river and through the trees, I felt I had just arrived in heaven. It was one of the most spectacular views I had ever seen. It was more than just the sights…there was such a feeling of happiness and joy that I could not explain.

I don't remember much of the interview with Hoffman. I remember the protest being heartfelt. There was a serious concern about the effects of the pumping on the Delaware. The protests led to a referendum vote in 1983 to dump the pump. However, in 1987 that vote was overturned by the courts. The pumping station was constructed and has been pumping out water ever since. It is ironic that the pumping did not avert the three recent disastrous floods.

My New Hope love affair started with that first trip. What followed were many trips to bed and breakfasts in the area. The 1740 House in Lumberville was a favorite. Each room had its own terrace overlooking the river. Just up the road was an old post office/general store/deli. A throwback to another age. So nostalgic and wonderful. Then up the road was the Black Bass Inn, famous for its collection of British Royalty memorabilia, along with good food and drinks. Near the inn was a small footbridge, great for a morning walk across the river.

Because I loved the area so much I decided it would be a terrific place to vacation. I browsed the *New York Times* Real Estate section and found a pool house for rent in New Hope. It was situated on the towpath just off Rabbit Run Bridge. I immediately called saying I would take the place sight unseen. The owner said she was having an open house on Saturday. I traveled from New York to New Hope early Saturday morning, hoping to be the first to view the property.

My trip down the narrow path to the towpath was frightening. It was a steep drop and barely seemed wide enough for a car to fit. That led to the property. On the three acres was a large modern house, grounds facing the Delaware River, and a path that led to a small bridge over a brook and onto to a large terrace with a beautiful inground pool and a small pool house.

The same feeling of joy I initially felt in New Hope had returned tenfold. I had to have this house. The owner said she had already accepted a check from a couple of guys. I prevailed upon her to take my check as the back up bidder just in case. A week later I received a call from the owner informing me that the initial check had bounced and if I wanted the house, it was mine for the season.

The years I rented that house were memorable. I even became comfortable driving down that steep drop to the towpath. The house was a magnet for my family and friends. We had a wonderful time just being together and exploring the area. There were boat trips on the river. My daughter and friends would go upriver, rent inner tubes, and ride down the river to our house. My son and his young daughter visited from California. When not doing our own cooking, we tried out the area restaurants. Favorites were The Raven, The Inn at Phillips Mill, Karla's, and the Cuttalossa Inn.

After three years, I was told the pool house would no longer be available. I was devastated, disheartened, disappointed. It was such a blow. After licking my wounds, I decided to search for a small place of my own—a place I could go to for weekend visits and summer vacations. After a few years of looking, I found and bought an enchanting one bedroom house in New Hope's Village Two. The house overlooked an expanse of primitive woods that stretched for miles. The complex contained a large pool, tennis courts, and a first-class French restaurant. It seemed ideal.

I continued my love affair with New Hope. Every time I crossed the bridge from Lambertville to New Hope, my heart would soar. I was happy to be coming home. The beauty in the area is something I try not to take for granted. The four seasons each offer something special. Sit in a restaurant like Martine's on a fall afternoon and look across at the magnificent mosaic of autumn colors surrounding the river . . . it's spectacular! Walk through the streets of Lambertville singing Christmas Carols on a cold winter's night, and it is a Norman Rockwell Christmas. Be anywhere in the Bucks County area during the season of spring when the gently rolling hills are covered with an infinite stretch of blossoming flowers …and you'll know it must be the closest thing to heaven.

When I retired in 1999, I decided to sell my house in Pelham, New York, and move full time to New Hope. It did not take me long to discover that my one bedroom New Hope townhouse was much too small for all of my belongings. As much as I loved that house, it just would not do. Because of the lack of space, my New York furniture had to be put into storage. After much soul searching, I decided to sell the townhouse and look for a bigger place. It never occurred to me to look anywhere else besides New Hope. What I found was a larger townhouse. When I first saw the house it wasn't even on the market yet, but I fell in love again. I knew I found exactly what I wanted and needed. It's a great house.

But what draws me to New Hope is much more than a house. It's really the people that make this place so special. Right from the start,

I felt so at home. My friends are wonderful. I rely on them, and I hope they know they can always rely on me. They have become my family in this enchanted place.

It has been twenty-six years since my first visit to New Hope. And yes, I've seen this town go through many changes—some good and some not so good...such as the many housing developments...I continue to believe there is something very special about New Hope. That's probably why so many people want to live where I love to live.

(For this former New Yorker, living in New Hope is truly a dream come true.)

Heaven on Earth

By Loretta DeGenova

My attraction to New Hope and the surrounding Bucks County area goes back more than forty years when my former husband and I, newly married, spent many memorable days driving our red sports car along River Road from Frenchtown to New Hope. We enjoyed shopping in the local quaint stores, dining in the charming restaurants, and ending the day dancing at the Cartwheel.

After divorcing, moving to New York City for a few decades, and summering in the Hamptons, I was still drawn back to the area a few weekends a year. I loved basking in the simplicity and charm of the local bed and breakfasts, savoring the atmosphere of the lush river's edge, and feeling myself transported to a setting reminiscent of the English Cotswolds. Twenty years older and wiser, I left a position working on the one-hundred-and-fifth floor of the World Trade Center and the hustle and bustle of New York City life. I accepted a local job as a school consultant. That was twelve years ago. Whether it is the ease and grace of daily life, the special friends, many of whom are transplanted New Yorkers, too, or the wonderfully diverse population that is the backdrop and pulse of New Hope, I have found a special home here.

I've been blessed to have lived in three diverse settings: one, an historical eighteenth-century miller's house with a pond and a few acres, which my Bouvier dog, Zoegirl, enjoyed exploring and where she is now buried; another house nestled in a place with different views of the Delaware River with its seasonal riverboats and where I enjoyed the sound of horse-drawn carriages clickety-clacking past my front porch (my friends would look in wonder at all of this and think it was too sweet to be true); and now in the lovely stone barn overlooking beautiful gardens and the many deer who cohabitate the land. I have finally come home to hear the inner voice of peace and know the moment-to-moment gifts and treasures of heaven brought to Earth!!!

Together We Can Make a Difference

By Reverend Charles J. Stephens

I love living near New Hope because of the progressive atmosphere this community brings to this whole area in both Bucks County, Pennsylvania, and Mercer County, New Jersey.

I came to this area when I was called to serve as the minister of the Unitarian Universalist Church at Washington Crossing in Titusville, New Jersey. My wife and our two children moved to this area from Concord, New Hampshire in 1997. Professionally, I felt drawn to serve the Unitarian Universalist Church at Washington Crossing because of the warm and welcoming quality of the members and the desire there was within the congregation to be a vibrant progressive force in the area. I believed that it had the potential to make numerous positive differences in individual lives and in the overall quality of life in the larger area.

At first, my wife, children, and I were simply attracted to the pleasure of walking around New Hope. As a community it offered us interesting and unusual shopping, dining, and entertainment possibilities. New Hope, of course, has the natural beauty of stretching out along the Delaware River. Since we live less than ten minutes away, New Hope quickly became one of the first places we would take our out-of-town visitors. We want our friends to experience New Hope because we know they, too, will enjoy what they find here and want to return often.

What I have come to love most about New Hope, however, is something that is at a much deeper level. New Hope brings a powerful progressive presence to our general area. The vision and mission of the Unitarian Universalist congregation which I serve is "the creation of an open and welcoming, caring religious community." Our congregation feels compelled to reach out to others because of our strong belief and the Unitarian Universalist principle of the inherent worth and dignity of every person and our deep desire for equity, justice, and compassion for all. We are totally committed to working hard in order to create a better world.

Ours was one of the very first official Unitarian Universalist "Welcoming Congregations." As such, we pride ourselves in being a liberal religious community that is open and welcoming to gays, lesbians, bisexuals, and transgender people. I have found in the New Hope community a strong ally and partner in promoting progressive and inclusive issues in general and especially in the area of LGBT rights.

I was excited when the New Hope Borough Council met to consider passing a comprehensive ordinance stating that New Hope does not discriminate on the basis of sexual orientation. I made sure that I was at the public council meeting the evening when people were invited to speak about the importance of that ordinance. Clearly, our congregation was pleased that the ordinance was passed. They were also pleased when they heard that I had spoken out in support of the ordinance.

Our Unitarian Universalist congregation enthusiastically marches in support of LGBT rights each year in the New Hope Celebrates parade. As I march along with others and look around at the crowds of people standing along the parade route, I am always thrilled to see the positive response from the people of all generations, colors, and orientations. It is a wonderful gathering of people who are there to celebrate equal rights for everyone, regardless of their sexual orientation.

I and the congregation I serve have long been strong advocates of gay marriages. The members of my congregation come from both New Jersey and Pennsylvania and they unanimously support the public stands I take in support of marriage equality for gay and lesbian couples.

My experience is that we, who are progressive in our principles, need allies if we want to reach our goals. As the minister of the Unitarian Universalist Church at Washington Crossing, so near New Hope, I have come to value the New Hope community highly. One person alone, one organization alone, and even a whole community alone cannot make major positive shifts in the thinking and in the behavior of society. It takes people and organizations working together in partnership.

What I have come to love most about New Hope is the community of people here who are ready and willing to join together to work for greater justice, equity, and compassion.

(Reverend Stephens's devotion to justice has led him to interfaith community organizing around many equity issues.)

Proud To Represent New Hope

By Chuck McIlhinney

As a lifelong resident of Bucks County, I have watched New Hope grow into one of the finest arts and cultural destinations in the state. Weekends find the downtown streets packed with people in town to enjoy the restaurants, arts, and entertainment. We have watched the town grow into the arts mecca of the East Coast, and the town's culture remains an important point of pride for the community. Despite the number of visitors, New Hope has not lost its small-town appeal and values. People are still friendly, kind, caring, compassionate, and considerate of others, and there is a strong sense of community that binds us together. The fact that the town has sustained its status as a tourist destination without compromising its small-town identity is a credit to the spirit and values of our citizens, and I continue to be amazed at the warmth and spirit of our people.

The diversity of the town is not limited to art galleries and antiques shops. Although most residents are not overly political, the people of New Hope hold a broad, moderate cross-section of opinions. Representing such a wide range of opinions is sometimes a difficult task, but it is made easier by the values that we all have in common, including respect for one another. The people of New Hope do not care if you are a Republican, Democrat, or belong to a third party, but they do care that you meet the needs of the community and make sure that every citizen is treated fairly. As a public official representing New Hope in our state capital, Harrisburg, I try to use this concept as a standard for every decision I make.

These decisions may not always be popular with my colleagues. One of my most memorable issues was consideration of legislation to prohibit same-sex benefits in Pennsylvania. I felt that this bill unfairly discriminated against the gay community. While the vast majority of my Caucus supported this legislation, I did not see the value in persecuting a certain group based on their beliefs. From my point of view, a vote for this bill was a vote for discrimination against a segment of the population that I am elected to serve.

This was not the popular opinion among some of my colleagues, and my opposition to the bill puzzled many of them. A fellow legislator asked me, "Why are you voting against this bill? Do you have that many gay people in your district?" "Maybe less than ten percent of my constituents are gay," I replied. "But this vote is also for the other ninety percent that are intolerant of intolerance."

I believe that most New Hope residents would echo this sentiment. We have a strong, tightly knit community, and taking away the rights of any segment of the community is the same as discriminating against the entire community. New Hope residents have captured the true spirit of community, and we are blessed to have that strength of resolve and dedication to one another. That is something that defines New Hope, and it is one of the most important reasons why I am proud to be its representative.

(Pennsylvania State Senator Chuck McIlhinney represents the 10th Senatorial District of Bucks and Montgomery Counties.)

Rainbow Room Does New Hope

By the Youth of Rainbow Room,
compiled by Marlene Pray

New Hope was the first public place where I didn't feel
    alone and scared.
It is like the Rainbow Room, but in an entire town.
It is a town built by lovers.
I stroll through this town of equality into breezy nights,
Sparkling window displays,
A smile inside.

I drive in from a rural, conservative community,
The realization of acceptance is overwhelming.
It is my home away from home.
Away from home,
The most, gay-happy place in Bucks County,
An oasis of support and love,
A great accepting town,
It truly is a new hope.

New Hope is peace and safety.
It gives me hope for the rest of Bucks County.
When will we learn?
I feel great when I go there and can be who I am
An awesome place to just be yourself.
It makes me happy because it is a place of love.

The best place to homosexually frolic!

The calm river brings beauty and peace,
Watching the ducks at the playhouse,
Great toys,
Rainbow flags and women holding hands,
Mmmm, El Taco Loco in my tummy.

We carried a hundred-foot flag through New Hope on Pride Day,
And I cried when people stood up and clapped for *me*—a queer youth.
So proud.
Thank you, New Hope.

(Founded in 2002 by Marlene Pray for Planned Parenthood Association of Bucks County in its Doylestown office, the Rainbow Room is Bucks County's only center for lesbian/gay/bisexual/transgender/queer/questioning/ allied youth between the ages of fourteen and twenty-one-years-old.)

Welcome to the Big Top, the Greatest Town on Earth

By Sharyn Keiser

Every day I am thankful and grateful that I moved with my partner, Sandy, to this special place full of beauty: beautiful people and a beautiful natural wonder with the river, canal, hills, and wildlife.

When first moving to New Hope, I had the privilege of living across the street from Philip Powell, with my rear yard cornering Doris Brandes's house, around the corner from Jim Martin, up the street from Ginger Shelley, and one block from Dorothy Grider. I became wealthy on the treasures of life experiences shared when spending time with these, as well as other, artistic jewels of New Hope.

And the breakfasts at Mother's Restaurant were fuel for the creative as well as the political and apolitical soul. The stories and the trips taken down memory lane by so many longtime New Hope residents were life lessons shared by an eclectic, wonderful cast of characters.

Whenever I had a weekday off from school, I would join the cast for breakfast. It was a very welcoming group. I was a newcomer back in the mid–1990s. Jim Martin was there everyday, Monday to Friday sitting in the same seat facing the sidewalk so he could see everything that was going on. Phil was there every weekday unless he was on one of his extended worldwide excursions that he took after a piece of his work was commissioned. You never knew which of the cast would stop in: Jim Carpenter, Tom Block, Ed Duffy, Elmer Case, Paul and Jan Witte, Allyson Kingsley, John Larsen, Joe Crilley, to name just a few.

And what a gift to be invited to Dorothy and Lydia's house for a glass of homemade wine, or a visit to Lydia's garden, or to Dorothy's studio to see her wonderful art and the children's books that she illustrated.

Being asked to have breakfast with the group that always went to the restaurant Duck Soup in Logan Square was quite an honor. What a fabulous group of artists and, more importantly, friends! John Larsen, Jack Rosen, and Joe Crilley held court discussing the world according to Joe, John, and Jack. And quite an interesting world that was!

New Hope remains a home to many of this cast of characters and many more wonderful family members. That is what is so special. You can differ in your opinions and beliefs, argue about things, and come back together, learn from one another's diverse perspectives, laugh, and live together in an incredible community.

I am grateful to have been introduced to New Hope by such a special group of people. I am thankful for all of the wonderful friends that I have made along the way and continue to make in my life's journey in New Hope. We are all artists creating our own unique canvas.

An Editor's Eye: In New Hope, the *Gazette* was the People's Paper

By Bridget Wingert

The old sign for the *New Hope Gazette* hangs on a wall in my house. It hung from the porch roof at the old *Gazette* office on Old York Road. It was not the paper's first office, but it served the *Gazette* well for almost forty years–before the operation moved downtown to Waterloo Street in 2000.

Advertising sales offices were near the front door and the editorial office was in the back, in what appeared to be a converted porch in the space above Melsons' Millbrook Farm, the restaurant supplier. The editor's office was delightfully bright all year round, but cold in the winter and hot in summer. You could set the clock by the New Hope & Ivyland trains that huffed past during the day and through the windows, you could see the steam train's smoke curling above the trees.

The most distinctive feature of the building was the smell of fish–a permanent odor from the downstairs market. The first person through the door in the morning tried to air the place a bit, but mostly we just got used to the fish smell.

It was an ideal location for a newspaper, with plenty of parking, easy access to New Hope and points north, south, and west, and it was relatively roomy. When I started working there the staff spoke proudly of the "all-girl *Gazette*." We had Kelly Bennett as ad manager, barely twenty at the time, but a super saleswoman; Jacqui Weber, another star; Patty Mangiaricina, yet another–the *Gazette* was the top income generator of the InterCounty Newspaper Group. Red-haired Ann Krisher was assistant editor and I was editor, starting in 1991.

At the front desk we had our elegant Hilde Wachtel, who came to New Hope via Vienna and New York. She was the receptionist, the person who sold classified ads, our fashion consultant, and the cultural leader. She was one of the founders of the Riverside Symphonia–John Michael Caprio's vision then as a professional orchestra serving the rivertowns. We celebrated Hilde's seventieth birthday at Gerry Krug's house in Pipersville and sometime during the party, we girls gathered for a chorus-line cheer of "G-A-Z-E-T-T-E."

We celebrated our uncorporate existence most Fridays around 4 PM with a bottle of wine, one time with caviar and crème fraiche. Hilde kept us spellbound with stories of World War II in Europe—her mother and younger brother were killed in the war. Nevertheless, Hilde was always upbeat. She was the morale builder, the charming woman who held us together.

The *Gazette* covered the floods and the snowstorms, the sudden encroachment of development on Solebury Township, and the crowding of the local schools as families moved in. Placing more than a hundred homes next to the 1970s Village 2 condominiums added to the school overflow. The Union Paper Mill closed down and reopened years later as Union Square, the office and shopping center. The community got behind the development of the James A. Michener Art Museum satellite in Union Square and the creation of Hardy Bush Way, a "back door" entrance to the town.

One frightening event in our town came from outside New Hope, and it was a direct affront to the welcoming community. In the early 1990s a neo-Nazi organization gained permission to march from South Main Street through the borough streets. And so they did, on a Sunday morning, storm troopers in black leather. Corporal Frank DeLuca, a longtime member of the New Hope police force, directed traffic, protecting the marchers at the Windy Bush intersection.

The *Gazette*'s relocation downtown was exciting. The office had carpeting and windows that looked out on the Delaware River. There, we could have our Friday gatherings on a porch outside, where we could watch the river. The office was high enough that floods did not directly affect it—at least not until 2006. Then the office closed for a few days because the street was impassable, but the archives survived.

We had a new sign installed at the front of the building on Main Street so I took the old one home with me. It is a pleasure to look at it and remember the *Gazette,* where I spent so many hours. It is a beautiful sign, showing artist Joseph Crilley's original masthead for the paper, which was first published in 1949.

That masthead was replaced in 2008 with a banner to match other newspapers in the InterCounty Group. Joe Crilley died this winter, and the *Gazette* closed soon after. It's a coincidence that few have noticed.

I was fortunate to work in New Hope when the *Gazette* was at its heyday. It was the "people's paper" and the community owned it before the bottom line became more important than the people.

(Bridget Wingert has been an editor or writer for Bucks County community newspapers for most of her life.)

Haiku

By Nevin Rae

"New Hope Seasons"

Spring

New Hope takes showers,
New Hope begins to blossom,
New Hope grows on me.

Summer

Over the bridges,
Along the ruby red path,
New Hope waits for me.

Fall

New Hope starts to wilt,
With a warm auburn color,
And loses its leaves.

Winter

Wintery landscapes,
Sidewalks like powdered sugar,
New Hope hibernates.

"Serenity"

Water rushing fast,
ducks waddle by with ducklings,
flowers by park bench.

*(Nevin is a New Hope-Solebury public school student. He has volunteered
with New Hope Arts and West End Farm, set up a Tibetan collection at
the New Hope-Solebury Library, and raised $15,000 for tsunami victims.
He has had private audiences with the Dalai Lama and President Bill
Clinton.)*

Came for the Summer…Stayed Forever

By Dee Rosenwald

I was asked how I came to live in the borough of New Hope, and to be frank, I came reluctantly and gradually at the time, some forty years ago. I was living and working at a job I loved in Manhattan, and I had vowed never again to leave New York City, not even for Paris or London. This aversion came about because I had spent ten previous years in Pound Ridge, New York, in northern Westchester County, in isolation on a rocky hillside amid fourteen acres of woodland where I brought up my son. I longed for a village or at least a friendly neighbor. We were pioneers in the fashionable exurbia of the 1950s. *Bah,* to that.

Now my new husband wanted to leave the city to return to bucolic Bucks County where he had once lived in an old mill and farmhouse in Rushland. He spoke fondly of the artists he had known here, how he played chess with Bill Ney on Mechanic Street, and shared time with sculptor, Harry Rosen, among others. For the summer of 1967, he rented the house on Waterloo Street where I still live.

So, I finally settled in a village of my dreams, and I found that it sparkled with creative people of all manner of creeds and genders. I was particularly intrigued by its significant history as this part of Pennsylvania was inherited by William Penn who created a colony of early Quaker settlers. They preserved and farmed the land and practiced their beliefs to live in peace and harmony with nature. In this county, we owe much to the "Friends" for their tolerance and charity to others; customs we have learned to follow and respect. Of course, General George Washington put us on the map during the Revolutionary War.

He marched through town and most certainly must have slept over before he crossed the Delaware.

New Hope's pride in its early history has inspired us to preserve old buildings. Presently we have more than one hundred on the Historic Register. Some have been transformed into popular restaurants. One is a former church. Now is that fun! In fact, we have become a culinary destination for gourmet diners. You cannot name another village in this county that can boast such a fine choice of dining spots. In addition, for those with a sweet tooth, we have an authentic French-owned patisserie with gateaux galore and fresh baked baguettes, and a Swiss family–owned confectionery from which pounds and pounds of handmade chocolates were shipped off to the White House this past January for the Obama Inaugural Celebration. How about that?

We are famous as an art center thanks to the turn of the last century's renowned Impressionist painters. Sadly, these days we have fewer artists in residence, studio space being at a premium. We do have lots of galleries and a new art center being expanded on Stockton Street under the guidance of Robin Larsen whose current endeavors provide us with an annual display of fine large sculptures throughout the borough.

Let's not forget our Bucks County Playhouse, made famous in the 1940s for its pre-Broadway openings. What could be a better treat for most village residents than to be within walking distance of live entertainment? Despite the endless revivals, the current company puts on darned good, spirited shows.

So finally, I must add to my list of things I like best about New Hope: Hurrah to the Farleys for keeping their bookshop open late in the evenings, proving that there are those among us who are bookworms!

(Dee Rosenwald has served for more than forty years as a member of the New Hope Historical Society and is well known for her annual motor coach tours.)

Harley Heaven

By Lance Simmens

Growing up in Philadelphia and relocating to Bucks County, Pennsylvania, in my teen years provided me with fond memories of New Hope. As a child in the late 1950s, I recall long Sunday afternoon car rides to the upper reaches of the greater Philly universe, landing in that idyllic riverside hamlet to observe beatniks huddled along the sidewalks playing guitars and bongos, and reading poetry. As a teenager in the 1960s, I ventured a shorter distance up River Road to smell the delicious, incense-fueled aroma of the various antiques and head shops, while the sidewalks were filled with tie-dyed, bell-bottomed, long hair hippies strumming guitars, sitting cross-legged, and flashing peace symbols in the familiar v-for-victory finger salute.

No trip to New Hope was complete without browsing through the now-closed Now and Then, the quintessential head shop located at the foot of the bridge connecting to Lambertville, New Jersey. Here one could purchase pipes and bongs, rolling papers, incense, posters of rock icons (such as Jimi Hendrix, the Doors, and Janis Joplin), black lights, or buttons proclaiming free love or the international peace symbol, while one was listening to psychedelic music. Later, I can vividly recall the hordes of leather-clad motorcycle gang members, wearing the colors of the Pagans, Warlords, and Hell's Angels, roaring through town. I watched with awe as these outlaws disembarked and strolled around as if reenacting a modern-day New Hope version of the Wild West. The only thing missing was the saloon with its swinging doors. The town gradually reverted to the artistic, eclectic nature that surely had been present all along: John and Peter's, where musical artists of Northeast

Corridor renown performed; the Bucks County Playhouse, where many aspiring actors and actresses paid their dues on the way to stardom; the mule path along the canal; and the various boutiques and restaurants tucked along the narrow side streets leading away from the Delaware River.

New Hope today is a mecca for middle-aged motorcyclists, like me, who showcase their finely polished machines, mostly Harley-Davidsons, in a peacock parade ceremony before their peers, comfortably positioned at Havana's. The open-air bar perched above South Main Street serves as a veritable fortress protecting the exit and entrance at the town's southern end. Through all my years, the town has held a fascination that changes along with the times. It is a place where all are welcome, where outrageousness is commonplace, accepted, and seemingly encouraged. It is a little slice of heaven wedged along the river. It is both a midpoint and a destination all in one. It is difficult to stop for less than an hour. In fact, on cool spring and fall days, it can entice visitors to stay much longer than they had planned.

The very name of the town itself evokes a feeling of renewal and promise. It is a place for all, and all are welcome. No trip to Bucks County is complete without a visit to this special town. I will always fondly remember this New Hope.

(Lance Simmens grew up in Bucks County and currently is Special Assistant to Governor Ed Rendell.)

A Little Corner of the World

By Eliana Young

My first experience with New Hope was in 1972 when I was nineteen-years-old and completely identifying with the Peace/Love movement. A friend of mine planned a short road-trip to this "really cool" place and, of course, I was "in," always ready for a new adventure. Although the details of that first visit are sketchy because so much time has gone by (and menopause has set in), I clearly remember the feeling, and all I can say is "Wow." It was like descending into a different energy field. Although it was only about an hour away from my suburban South Jersey neighborhood, this little town was worlds away in its vitality. The streets swarmed with an eclectic crowd largely made up of long-haired bohemian types strolling past head shops, record stores, quaint little restaurants, and small nightclubs. I remember that John & Peter's had just opened, and we couldn't wait to check it out. New Hope was a mecca for art, music, and theater, all crammed into the few blocks that made up the little downtown area. It was inspiring, and I found that I, too, wanted to write and paint and create. I thought I had discovered "San Francisco East."

The diversity and accepting spirit of the town were also striking. I remember going into Mother's, which, if memory serves me, was just a sweet shop at the time. I overheard the counter staff talking and from their conversation, I could tell they were openly gay. Unfortunately, that was something people did not talk about in my circle of friends (homosexuality wasn't removed from the official list of mental disorders until 1973). Even though everyone I knew considered themselves "open," being gay still had too much stigma for comfort. But from what I could tell, in this little haven, it seemed to be just another normal lifestyle. In short, I remember feeling very much at home here, yet I never thought this area would be "my home." I was busy going to college and having fun. I knew I would visit again and again, as I have over the years, but where I would settle down wasn't even a blip on the radar.

The years went by and I lived my life, maturing to a degree (at least in my opinion), shedding the mindset of being on a perpetual vacation and reluctantly taking on the responsibilities of an adult. I continued to visit New Hope often, having my favorite rituals, like getting the "after–Thanksgiving Day turkey" sandwich at Havana's (until I learned about factory farming), indulging in a double-scoop at Gerenser's Exotic Ice Cream and strolling at least once around Now and Then—even years after my bell-bottom jeans and fringe jacket had been laid to rest.

As time went on and fighting the wrath of gravity became a necessary undertaking, exercise became an important part of my life. At that point I began to see New Hope and its sister-town, Lambertville, in a completely new light. Biking and walking on the canal path became one of the most restorative activities I could imagine. Traveling down the towpath helped me get centered.

Many times I would find myself admiring the houses that backed up to the canal, and I would fantasize about living in one of them, but had no plans or real expectations of ever moving to the area. I was more of a free spirit, and my home base was a place to sleep, eat, and change clothing. I really wasn't home that much. That remained true until a friend introduced me to the perfect stranger. I quickly felt my withered roots begin to grow. We moved in together almost immediately and soon bought a wonderful townhouse in West Trenton, New Jersey. For the first time I got into the whole nesting thing and just fell in love with my house. It was truly my first home as an adult, and we were very happy there. My partner continually expressed an interest in moving to Lambertville, but I was so content, I could not even consider it. She did not give up.

Almost every spring, she would go on a "move to Lambertville" campaign, looking at houses for sale and coercing me into car rides around town. She couldn't understand why I was so resistant because she knew it was my kind of place. Honestly, she was right. I had known that the first time I laid eyes on the area. I guess I became so attached to the feelings and the happy memories we created in the townhouse that I just did not want to let any of that go. So year after year, I'd wait it out, and summer would distract her until the next year. "Phew," another one down. I never wanted to move.

However, you can never say "never." Sometimes life takes an unanticipated turn that forces fate. In this case, it was my mother moving in with us. It took only a short time before we realized that in order for my mother to be truly comfortable and to feel at home, she needed her own space. So, I came to terms with the fact that I needed to leave my little sanctuary and buy a house that had living quarters for my mother. Once my mind was made up, I took up the search full force and headed straight to the New Hope/Lambertville area. It was the only place that made sense. I had always loved it; my partner loved it; we had dear friends there; it was beautiful and much more. Rather than bore you with the details, I will just say that we found a wonderful house right on the towpath in Lambertville. One of those houses I had fantasized about. I absolutely love everything about it. Once again, my partner was right. She is wise beyond her years, and I say that not just because I'm crazy about her. The longer we are together, the more I realize that nine-and-a-half times out of ten, she's right, especially when she says, "We didn't just buy a house; we bought a lifestyle." To the delight of that restrained bohemian child who still lives inside of me, I feel like I am on a perpetual vacation. We live in a resort area where you can walk outside your door and go to some of the best restaurants in the tri-state area, enjoy the arts, shopping, and antiquing, or just take in nature.

What I love most about this area is the energy and the people. It's the kind of place where statements aren't necessary because you can just be yourself. Be funky, be straight, be gay, be whatever it is that is the art of being you. This type of open attitude gives way to the undeniable creative energy of the area. Although, like many of us, these sister-towns have become more mainstream, they maintain an extraordinary charisma, which draws in all types of people. That is what gives them such an exceptional spirit.

In short, I thank God for guiding me here, a little corner of the world where I feel that I belong. A place that still makes me want to paint and write and create. A place where the people are always interesting and the options are endless. A place where each day has all the right stuff for a new adventure. Carpe diem!

New Hope—Inside and Out

By Roy Ziegler

Long ago, I stopped counting the times that people have told me how lucky I am to live in New Hope, Pennsylvania. Over the past eight years as a volunteer guide for the New Hope Historical Society, I have been privileged to lead numerous tours of this historic, picture-perfect town. I have personally interacted with literally thousands of folks from all over the world whose travels led them to New Hope.

What a pleasure it is for me to observe the fascinated expressions on their faces as I relate our rich history and shepherd them around our streets, historic buildings, parks, canal towpath, and riverbank. The first Lenni-Lenape people settled here about 10,000 years before William Penn came and authorized the sale of land with the requirement that this community be established. And it isn't just that George Washington slept here; he actually led 10,000 troops of the Continental Army through this town, and his troops prepared for the Battle of Trenton here!

The visitors' amazement and enthusiasm enhance my deep affection for this unique place, an affection that I cannot fully describe. Perhaps it was best expressed by the first president of the New Hope Historical Society, Dr. Arthur J. Ricker, about fifty years ago when he said, "… there is an "indefinable" something that embraces one's mind and spirit with a warm feeling of graciousness, reverence, humility, and pride in what we call our …heritage." Indeed, Dr. Ricker was the catalyst who helped to preserve our rich history. He led the way toward the preservation of more than one hundred structures in New Hope that have graced this historic town for more than two hundred years.

On another score, I have been privileged to be an active member of two borough government committees. These groups are composed of concerned and dedicated residents who devote a lot of their personal time contributing to the improvement and revitalization of New Hope. This is a concept that those fascinated visitors would be hard-pressed to understand. Those of us who are fortunate to call this town "home" know how very much time is needed to preserve, maintain, and enhance this great community. Our discussions are often heated, sometimes acrimonious, but always with the end view that we want this town to be better than it was before we arrived. We see the imperfections and the signs of a venerable town that demand our attention and action. Our passionate feelings about New Hope drive us.

I am heartened by the volunteers who turn out on sub-freezing, inclement Saturday mornings to help decorate the town for the holiday season; stunned by the overwhelming generosity of this community in its support of disaster victims, preservation of historic buildings, and promotion of the arts; astounded by the willingness of our most-macho first-responders and government officials to dress in drag for shows to promote community events; and pleased that our town embraces and celebrates diversity regardless of religious beliefs, sexual orientation, political persuasion, race, or ethnicity.

My two ongoing, somewhat polar, roles in this community help to balance my appreciation for all that is great about New Hope. On the one hand, I observe with great pleasure the enjoyment experienced by thousands of visitors as they tour this terrific place; on the other, I am part of a passionate group of residents whose aim is to keep it that way and maybe, even, make it a better place for greater fascination and quality of living.

As I have replied to many folks that I have met over the years, "Yes, I am truly fortunate to be living in New Hope, Pennsylvania."

(Roy Ziegler is author of the new book, New Hope, Pennsylvania—River Town Passages.*)*

Feels Like Home

By Annette Katona Rosenberg

I arrived in New Hope in the late 1980s to work as a sales manager at the Holiday Inn which was located on Route 202—right on the fringes of downtown New Hope. As I drove to my new job that first day, I had the clear feeling that I was "home." I instantly felt a connection to this new environment that was so comforting. My job was to drum up business for the hotel—to sell its facilities, rooms, conference halls, restaurant and banquet facilities, et cetera. In essence, I had to sell New Hope. What a treat that was for me!

I became very active in the community, local chambers of commerce, and tourist boards throughout Bucks County and the Philadelphia area. I had success in selling accommodations at the Holiday Inn because it was situated in such a great location…New Hope. I remember meeting people who were spending a whole week of their summer vacation with us. At first I was somewhat baffled by this…seven days with the entire family in New Hope, Pennsylvania? I quickly learned that just a week in this area would barely give you enough time to skim the surface. There is literally no end to the abundance of attractions in the Bucks County region: museums, art galleries, live entertainment, historic houses and battlefields, shops galore, a local winery, an old-fashioned steam locomotive, mule-drawn barge rides, ghost tours, and hot air balloon trips, just to name a few. For the outdoor enthusiast, I was quick to point out all of the opportunities for canoeing, biking, hiking, tubing, and boat rides on the Delaware River. I used to tell my potential clients, "Stay for as long as you like. I can guarantee that you'll never run out of things to do."

In the dead of winter when tourism was naturally at a low level, the Holiday Inn decided to produce a Murder Mystery Dinner Theater. We engaged local shops and attractions to be part of this event as "clue locations." People absolutely loved this "Whodunit" event! It was a smashing success and is still talked about to this day.

I was so taken with all the wonderful things that New Hope has to offer visitors that I decided to open a business on Main Street called the Tourist Trap. The concept of this retail shop was to sell New Hope souvenirs along with an array of other items that were made in or around Bucks County. I also added wicker baskets to my inventory, which gave the store a very unique feel. I made friends with customers from near and far who would make it a habit to stop into the store on their return visits to New Hope even if it was just to say, "Hi." It was fascinating to meet people from all over the world. At times, a purchase made at my store might be a foreigner's first experience in dealing with U.S. currency.

I remained active in tourism working for Peddler's Village, in nearby Lahaska, in their marketing department. This enabled me to keep my tourism connections with New Hope as well. Eventually, I was able to purchase the building that housed my Tourist Trap business. My good fortune continued, and I went on to buy the business next door to me called Pretzel Benders. These two business acquisitions sealed my future in New Hope.

For three years (1988–1991), I served on the board of directors for the New Hope Chamber of Commerce. We accomplished many positive things for the town, but one thing in particular stands out in my mind. We were able to bring a section of the AIDS Memorial Quilt to New Hope. We had pieces of the quilt displayed in various shops along Main Street. I cannot express in words what an incredibly moving and poignant experience this was. The quilt (which is known as the longest ongoing community arts project in the world) is a beautiful symbol of remembrance, awareness, and hope.

After spending so much time among the many gifted and talented inhabitants of New Hope, it wasn't long before I felt the urge to take a creative plunge myself. I was lucky enough to attend New York University where I took a weekly class in the business and craft of television writing. I even became a member of the New York chapter of Television Arts and Sciences.

So many people from all walks of life have touched my heart here in New Hope. I have made lifelong friends who feel like family. I met, fell in love with, and married my soul mate, Alan Rosenberg, who was living just a few doors away on Main Street. We have been blessed with a wonderful daughter who will have the privilege of growing up in such a richly diverse community surrounded by many special friends who have touched her life.

I am so proud to live in a town where friends, neighbors, visitors, and strangers can thrive in an atmosphere that fosters and celebrates freedom and individuality. The next time you see the crowds flocking into our town on a weekend, remember why they are here. They have come because they want to spend some of their precious free time in our little corner of the world. They come because they know that this little town will embrace them with wide arms, an open mind, and a welcoming heart.

I am truly lucky to have found my "home" where neighbors are friends, and friends are like family. As someone once said, "Home is the one place in the entire world where hearts are sure of each other." I am so grateful that I have been able to call New Hope my home.

Our New World Camelot

By Barry Ziff

Often I refer to New Hope as Camelot. No, it is not the New World location for the Round Table with knights in shining armor. Nor is it the place where Sir Galahad will start his search for the Holy Grail. I certainly am not aware of a Merlin-clone who will produce magical feats. But New Hope is a place that is associated, in my mind, with a "Vale of Magic" that qualifies it as the New World Camelot.

Early on, I noticed that many New Hope residents seem to live long, active years. My unofficial, unscientific survey required my reading the obits in the now-defunct New Hope *Gazette*. I used the age of eighty as a life bellwether. Then I added the pros (many) and cons (few) of the town.

Cons: the winter season, overpriced cocktails, floods, and property taxes.

Pros: virtually everything else about living in New Hope.

During the early 1970s, my wife, Sallie, and I discovered wonderful, giving, helpful friends, acquaintances, and strangers. The mingling of the various adult age groups adds to the vitality of the community. I believe that this mixture helps us enjoy a longer life. Our environment, which incorporates the river, canal, rolling hills, and the four seasons, adds to the quality of life. One must also consider the historical nature of our town. The history of the New Hope community is intertwined and complemented by all the arts. Our small town has the feel of a part-urban world in a country setting.

The following story is about our wonderful New Hope friends and the four major floods of 1996, 2004, 2005, and 2006. After our home purchase in 1980, I unfortunately joked that "if you live *on* the river, you should expect to live *in* the river." We have been swimming in the river from the first week we moved in, but we did not think its waters would overwhelm us. Could we have been in flood denial? Local, knowledgeable people warned us that Mother Nature could not be controlled. "Expect to be flooded," they said. We took that chance. We were young and somewhat misinformed. We knew that a major flood had occurred in 1955, and the big flood before that, in 1936.

During the cold, snowy January of 1996, we experienced the lack of preparation by the Army Corps of Engineers. There was a delayed response to the ice peril on the Delaware River. The river-spanning bridge at Port Jervis, New York was threatened, and we had heard that the ice dam had been dynamited. The rumor was that a fourteen-and-a-half foot wall of ice and water was racing toward us and evacuation was our best option.

Prior to the evacuation notice, we foolishly attempted to pump out the water that was encroaching upon the basement. We had one working pump. Our friends Jurgen Schweickhardt and John Bayma loaned us a second pump. The pumps could not defeat the river. Our next step was, along with Jurgen, John, and our son Mark, to move the first-floor furnishings to our second floor, out of harm's way. We took refuge at Jurgen and John's home.

The next morning we visited our flooded home. Our "Vale of Magic" prevailed. We were spared first-floor water damage, but we suffered approximately a foot-and-a-half flood in the basement. That made sense. New Hope's flood stage is thirteen feet; add one-and-a-half feet of icy cold, damaging river water, and that equals the fourteen-and-a-half foot rumor.

While pondering our next move, Borough Councilmen Fred Williamson and Jake Fell did an inspection visit. Their safety-related question was about the heater and electrical panel location. When we showed them the dry first floor where the utilities in question were located, they gave us a "good to proceed" blessing. Breakfast was served at the Holiday Inn that morning and it seemed all was well.

Sallie's most accommodating family showed up to give us a clean-up helping hand. That was great, particularly since I had experienced bypass surgery the previous May. My health was returning at a snail's pace. I could not really sustain any heavy-duty work activity. I barely assisted with the clean-up process. Thankfully, our losses were minimal. The "Vale of Magic" was working.

Foolishly, we thought that flooding had been ended for a long time. A major flood occurred in 1904. The next big flood was 1936. That was a thirty-two-year period. After 1936, the next really big flood was the 1955 monster. There were just nineteen years between those two floods. Since the reservoirs were built on the tributaries of the Delaware, we felt confident that we had paid our dues with the 1996 flood.

Surprise, surprise. We were not aware of, at that time, the misguided services of the Delaware River Basin Commission (DRBC). Through the lack of positive action and lack of anticipation by the DRBC, we have had three floods in less than two years—2004, 2005, and 2006. Each flood incident caused a higher degree of panic within our souls. How did we keep our sanity? It was not an easy situation to live with.

But that "Vale of Magic" returned with each episode. When the flooding occurred, the magic returned with the help from neighbors, friends, relatives, acquaintances, and even total strangers. New Hope and Solebury residents appeared every time to ask how they could help.

For each flood, Susan White took Jennie Dog to her home. Abigail Leavitt was in charge of rescuing my messy desk. Pennsylvania Assemblyman Bernie O'Neill, former Council President Richard Hirschfield, and Mayor Larry Keller had dumpsters placed in convenient locations for all of the flood victims. The garage was power-washed by members of a local Buddhist Temple. Tom, Michael, and Alycia Scannapieco brought members from their church to assist with our problem. Kurfiss Sotheby's International Real Estate agents lead by Michael Richardson showed up with Cecily Laidman in tow to come to our assistance. Guardian angels Ned Irons and his friend Ray Kinloch often worked nonstop doing everything from moving furniture, to power-washing. They also provided a generator and hoses so that we, and our neighbor Dr. Claire Shaw, had clean water for personal use. They hooked up the hose to the home of David Oess and Bill Keifer. David and Bill are our Angels of Mercy who also moved furniture and handled the electric and utility problems. Bryce and Jane Sanders provided us with living quarters for six days along with onsite assistance. Larry

Emmertz corrected the position of our heating oil tank from floating to stable. The efforts of Roland van Dommelan, Jurgen Schweickhardt, and John Bayma were also appreciated. Those three weeks were the hardest times of our lives; however, the support received from neighbors and friends was the greatest consolation.

The New World Camelot does exist. The "Vale of Magic" lives within the souls of these and other wonderful residents who assisted us and helped others during the flooding along the beautiful banks of the Delaware River. Finally, our knowledge of our diverse community shows a melding of many kinds of people of every age group, religion, and type of life partner. Being supportive in times of stress was a glorious life choice for those who helped. This story shows the spirit of New Hope. It is why we hope to stay here for the best of our lives.

Caring and Charming Rivertown

By Bernie O'Neill

New Hope has a long and rich history. It provides a unique and quaint lifestyle for many, offers a dazzling array of entertainment, and the quantity of natural resources sets this Delaware River town on a canvas of breathtaking beauty. From its significance as the home of the Lenni-Lenape people to the establishment of the essential grist and corn mills, New Hope continues to thrive as a mecca for modern-day adventurers.

New Hope's spectacular beauty, ambiance, and riverside playhouse are known globally. Who can resist the charm of its narrow, winding streets better suited for horses and buggies than for automobiles; the mule-drawn barges; historic steam engine train rides, and river scenes? The faces, names, and voices of those who have lived and worked in New Hope make it extraordinary among our state's and our nation's rivertowns. The Founding Fathers, George Washington and William Penn, actress Grace Kelly, choreographer Bob Fosse, and singer/songwriter Paul Simon are just a few of the many famous people who have walked its streets.

In the past six years, as I have served as state representative for New Hope Borough, the thing that stands out in my mind about this community is that New Hope's greatest asset is its people. From shopkeepers, teachers, council members, and artists to the local firefighters, historical society volunteers, restaurateurs, real estate agents, and nurses, everyone contributes to making New Hope a special place to live, work, raise our families, and enjoy a little R&R.

New Hope residents care about their town in a way that should make everyone proud. I saw that high level of caring in 2004, 2005 and 2006 when the waters of the Delaware overflowed their banks and sent water into dozens of homes and businesses. During the aftermath of each of the three floods, I saw volunteers helping homeowners remove debris, business owners doing everything they could to reopen in a timely fashion, and first responders and local officials helping people clean up and plan to prevent future destruction.

Even after the floods repeated themselves, everyone truly came together and showed their compassion and spirit for New Hope. Helping one another did not just mean pulling together to assist their neighbors, it meant rebuilding a town and renewing a tradition that was founded upon centuries of time and generations of families.

But it's not just the challenging times that bring New Hope citizens together. Each year, people from hundreds of miles around come together for the Winter Festival, the Shad Festival, the New Hope Auto Show, the Outdoor Arts and Crafts Festival, and to visit nationally acclaimed inns and restaurants. In recent times, New Hope Celebrates has become an annual event celebrating diversity in a town where everyone is welcomed all year round. It takes an enormous amount of work to organize and prepare for the festivals and special events, and those New Hopers who lend a hand exhibit a 150 percent level of determination and pride. Thank you to all of our many, many volunteers and event coordinators for continuing to make New Hope such an outstanding destination for visitors from around the world.

In my travels around Pennsylvania, I have encountered many people who have come to New Hope and who speak highly of their visits. Many come frequently and have fallen in love with the town—as I have—and keep returning to partake in new adventures. Whether spending time in New Hope to connect with nature, support the arts, spend a romantic weekend, or escape the hustle and bustle of a busy life along the East Coast, both residents and visitors have found this quaint little hamlet to be unique among tourist destinations. One cannot take a stroll down Main, Bridge, Mechanic or Ferry Streets without passing the dozens of family-owned businesses that make up the heart and soul of New Hope's commercial district. The art galleries, gift shops, clothing stores, bookshop, and restaurants comprise a network where each business brings out the very best in one another.

Every day, and in every way, residents and business owners work together to ensure that their town retains its eighteenth-century charm while thriving in the twenty-first century.

(State Representative Bernie O'Neill is a member of the Pennsylvania House of Representatives, 29th Legislative District.)

The Perfect Blend

I have been a part of the New Hope community for over thirty years. Clearly, this is the place where my heart feels at home.

"Why?" you ask.

Wow! It's hard to answer that question because there is so much that makes this town great. But the ultimate answer lies in one word, "community." New Hope is filled with the most amazing people in the world, and they are the ones that make this place work.

Way back in the 1970s when I was a college student in Manhattan, I came to visit one of my favorite uncles, Uncle Paul, who had been living here for years, and that did it. I decided that New Hope was the place for me. I have lived here with my partner for three decades now. We have also become business partners and things have worked out smoothly and successfully for both of us.

There is no doubt about it—New Hope is a wonderful place. A few people say that over the years the town has lost some of its luster, but I disagree. I say that it has aged quite nicely into a terrific mix of people. We have a great combination of folks who are able to keep alive an atmosphere that is a perfect blend of being both sophisticated and free-spirited.

Back in the "good ol' days" (now that's an old-fashioned expression), there used to be a slew of fun nightclubs in the area. We had a grand time hopping around from one place to another. Sadly, those nightclubs have gone away, but the diversity and the fun continue.

For the past five years, I have been a board member of the New Hope Chamber of Commerce, as well as serving as the past president.

It has been a privilege and a pleasure to be able to interact with all of the people, businesses, and organizations that make our town so unique. Our local government was one of the first boroughs to enact a non-discrimination ordinance in Pennsylvania. Kudos to us! We also created New Hope Celebrates (NHC), an organization that supports the gay, lesbian, bisexual, and transgender populace and professional community. Many other fine organizations have provided environmental leadership and awareness for our town.

New Hope is blessed with natural beauty, a unique atmosphere, and most of all, with hard-working and caring people. We need to step back and look at who we are and what we have achieved. We're a little town with a big heart. I feel so lucky to call New Hope my home.

Certainly Embraced Me

By Rhea Rawley

My first experience in New Hope was in the late 1960s. My sister had just gotten her first car, had a paycheck in her hand, and was ready to get as far away from the Jersey Shore as a tank of gas and a few hours of driving time would take her. My family wasn't big on traveling and felt that the ocean and the Steel Pier provided all the entertainment a teenage girl could want. And if you needed to "venture out" you could drive down the Garden State Parkway to Wildwood.

However, my sister had her sights set on someplace called "New Hope," and after much cajoling and promises of not making any detours or picking up any hitchhikers, my folks conceded. *BUT* she had to agree to take me along for the trip. They told her they did not want her to travel alone, but I think they felt that if she took me along, she couldn't get into too much trouble. You see, my sister was eight years older than I, which placed me in Junior High—old enough to be able to tell the police my name, phone number, and address, should we end up in a horrific car accident and my sister was rendered unconscious. And young enough to be a crimp in any plans that she might have that could lead her into the path of temptation.

My sister agreed to all their rules, and bright and early on a sunny Saturday morning we were off—windows down, radio blasting, two single women out on a big adventure. Well, one single woman and one very impressionable kid, but we were free. We sang the sonnets of Jim Morrison and talked about which Beatle we thought was the cutest. She loved John and I argued that George was the unsung hero of the group. I secretly loved John too, but hey, what's a road trip without an argument or two?

When we reached the bridge between Lambertville and New Hope, we both knew we were about to make the leap between the security of New Jersey and the unknown in the great state of Pennsylvania. At the end of this metal bridge, which spanned the mighty Delaware, was New Hope. I did not know what to expect. All I knew was that it was somewhere my sister wanted to go. Not just wanted to go, needed to go. Some place that she needed to see and if it was good enough for her, it certainly was good enough for me.

When we got across the bridge, I sensed that we were in a different world. We parked the car, got out, and just sort of stood there looking around. There were hundreds of young people in blue jeans and brightly colored, gauzy shirts. Everyone had long hair; some with headbands, some with flowers, and some in big Afros that you knew would be long if they weren't so fluffy. There were people singing, playing guitars, and dancing. They all seemed seriously engaged in the act of being joyful. "Joyful" was not a word that I could use to describe much in Atlantic City, but it certainly was the perfect word to describe New Hope. My sister immediately reached down and took off her penny loafers. I could sense that she had crossed a threshold, she was transforming. She rushed me into a tiny shop where she bought earrings with peace signs, a leather-fringed headband, and a wristband that matched. Barefoot and adorned in her sunglasses, and hippie accessories, she "fit in."

People on the street were giving us the peace sign. Were these Communists? Were these the anarchists my father ranted about, that would be the destruction of this country with their dope-smoking, peace-loving commie ways? They didn't seem so bad. A little hairy and a little grimy maybe, but they all seemed happy and carefree. They did not seem scary at all.

What really impressed me was that I suddenly felt very different. I was content. I was calm. I was peaceful. I was in a magical place that could instantly embrace you and make you feel safe, even if only for a short while. I also knew that I would be coming back!

In the late 1970s, I made my second trip to New Hope. I had just gotten my first car and what more fitting way to break it in than to go to New Hope? My four friends and I piled into my 1965 baby blue Rambler and set out for an adventure of our own.

There was that same old metal bridge that was the pathway from the same old New Jersey into the magical world of New Hope. Some changes had taken place over the years. Folks in hip-hugger jeans and beat-up army jackets replaced the brightly dressed people of the 1960s. There was still the long hair and peace signs, but the gaiety of the sixties seemed to have been replaced with a little cynicism. After all, we were just coming out of a very nasty, controversial war, were experiencing some tough economic times complete with long gas lines and unemployment. But when I opened the car door, that same calm and contentedness came back. I knew that this was where I needed to be at that moment in time. My friends had never been to New Hope, so I, as the old pro, took the lead and could not wait to show them all the magic that this little town possessed.

We wandered in and out of all the shops. We were enamored with the old buildings with narrow staircases, crammed full of handmade masterpieces. We talked with many of the shopkeepers who seemed to enjoy the opportunity to show off their crafts, discussing who had made what and how a certain something had been created in such a way that you could distinguish that individual's work from another.

We learned more about arts and crafts than we ever did in art class. We ate lunch at the Towpath Restaurant on Mechanic Street. Here is where I believed I had spent another life. The sound of the stream and the sight of the lush green brush combined with the subtle smell of old structures and good cooking stole my heart. I knew from that moment on that New Hope was where I belonged. My friends and I made a pact that we would come back to this place once a year and we did! I also came back with other friends and sometimes by myself, but I kept coming back.

In the late '80s and '90s, I came to New Hope with new friends. Friends that I met at work; some were my bosses, and some were coworkers. All knew that New Hope was something special. All, at one time or another, spoke of opening a little shop here. But it wasn't until 2002, after I had been "downsized," which I believe was also being called "upscaling" by the demons of downsizing, that everything changed. After years of sitting around my dining room table, drinking beers, eating pizza, playing cards, and talking about opening a shop in New Hope, my boss put my hand to the fire and put my money where my mouth was. She had already been transferred to Blue Bell, Pennsylvania. She convinced me to sell my townhouse, move in with her, and open the shop of our dreams. After a year of working out our business plan and spending a lot of time talking with other shop owners, we opened the doors of Not Too Shabby in February 2003.

Our first location was next to the New Hope & Ivyland Railroad station. The shop was wonderful. One side faced the train and the other faced the canal. How perfect to look out your window and watch the ducks and the geese raising their babies. Several times a day the mule barge would come down the canal. The mule barge is a tourist attraction today, complete with a banjo player and a guide pointing out places of interest. The canal played an integral part in New Hope's history, moving cargo and coal.

While this location for our shop was fine, we felt like we really weren't a part of what we knew New Hope to be. After two years and with the help of one of the many friends that we had made, we found a spot on North Main Street, the breath of New Hope.

What I learned from my time spent in New Hope is that this is a town that reaches out and grabs you. It doesn't care if you are gay or straight, young or old, rich or poor, colorful or colorless, human or animal; it wraps its arms around you and embraces your soul. This little town is only about one square mile in size, but it is jam-packed with about two hundred and eighty shops, restaurants, and galleries. It has the Bucks County Playhouse, a mule barge, a ferryboat, carriage rides, and ghost tours. New Hope has a towpath for romantic walks on the canal. It snuggles up to the Delaware River and is steeped in history, as it is only a short span from where Old George crossed it on that icy Christmas Day.

More importantly than any of this, New Hope has soul. It is a warm embrace, a belly laugh, a pat on the back, a kick in the ass, a carnival, a blank canvas, a home, and a heart. In these trying times, nothing beats a place like New Hope.

John Larsen

By Robin Larsen

"One day, while relaxing on the patio at John & Peter's, a young man asked me if I remembered the 'good old days.' I told him that I did and asked when he thought the good old days were."

" 'Oh, about six or seven years ago,' he said."

"I listened, realizing that for most of us the good old days began around the time that each of us moved to New Hope. Stay long enough and you come to realize that the 'magical' good old days don't really exist at all. The good old days are now and yesterday and tomorrow."

Thus flows the wisdom of John Larsen—who has lived in this community for fifty years and who is the founder of one of the best-known music clubs on the East Coast. Although he is now considered a pillar of the creative community, he did not begin his career here.

Born in Denmark and raised most of his life in a New York orphanage, he began his adult journey in the Navy at age seventeen. Like so many men his age, the G.I. Bill allowed him to pursue an education and his love of acting at the University of Miami and later City College in New York. But with marriage and family came a growing awareness of reality and responsibility, and he abandoned theater and migrated to Philadelphia, Doylestown, and finally to New Hope.

It is in New Hope that he left his executive persona behind and returned to his New York roots, opening a bohemian, Greenwich Village–type of coffee house. No drums, no liquor, but lots of 1960s conversations and chess. From the beginning, John's Place, as it was first known, had a respect for original music and the comfortable feel of a living room.

Over the years, John & Peter's has changed as New Hope has changed. Always a local favorite, home to numerous benefits for artists, the community, and causes—political activist Abbie Hoffman was a fixture—rarely a month goes by when the club is not raising money for a musician or an artist in need. The community has always been an integral part of its success, and it has progressed with the new interests and ideas of the patrons. The intimate stage has been home to everyone from folk purist Odetta to the new, young voices of internationally popular WEEN.

If the music is original and the musicians dedicated, they will likely find acceptance and a stage at the famous New Hope nightspot. A stop into the club reveals walls covered with posters (many hand-drawn by local artists) of performers such as Mary Chapin Carpenter, Penn & Teller, Norah Jones, and other great blues and rock performers, all of who have played the intimate room. Take a quick glance around, and you will be amazed by the myriad of locally created, stained-glass windows and lights, and the mini-gallery of local painters' works.

But if the music is the mission, it is the people who have kept the longest-running club on the East Coast hopping. Known as the place that never closes—it is open three-hundred-and-sixty-five days of the year with music every day and twice on Saturdays and Sundays. The club has been historically the last to close and the first to open after a flood. And the staff has been known to serve by candlelight when the power goes out. They have rolled with the good times and bad, musicians now play drums and synthesizers, alcohol is served, and the name changed to John & Peter's when partner Peter Price joined the team. However, John Larsen remains—thirty-eight years after he embarked on a dream that became a mainstay of New Hope.

In between, he has served as head of the Restaurant Association, the Chamber of Commerce, Chairman of the Zoning Hearing Board, and as head of the original New Hope Arts and Crafts Show where he met me, Robin, his wife of twenty-five years. At eighty-two-years of age, John is hardly one to dwell on the past. Still at work every day and still active in a number of organizations, including my project, The New Hope Arts Center, he continues to look to the future and to listen to new ideas and new music. Always proud to be part of the warm, welcoming, inclusive arts community that he helps to define, John remembers the "good old days"—just like they were yesterday.

(Robin Larsen is the Executive Director of the New Hope Arts Center.)

Progressing to New Hope

By Howard Savin

It was fall 1974 when I first visited New Hope, Pennsylvania. I had moved to the state the previous summer with my wife and two young children to begin an internship in clinical psychology in a facility located on Philadelphia's Main Line. Friends had told us that New Hope was a great place for day trips with its wide array of art galleries, crafts shops, restaurants, and a colorful cast of interesting, "offbeat" citizenry. This began a progression of events that led to becoming a full-time resident of the New Hope-Solebury area twenty-two years later. The initial visit was a big success. The kids ate pizza and we all enjoyed the festive atmosphere. Music wafted onto the street, everyone seemed friendly, and the stores were unique, which made it fun to browse and shop—even for me, a card-carrying non-shopper. In fact, this exposure to Bucks County resulted in a subsequent move to Doylestown to join a private practice.

For years we lived in Doylestown and spent more and more weekends and evenings in New Hope, enjoying the restaurants, clubs, and shops with family and friends. A growing number of our out-of-town friends wanted to stay with us and visit New Hope. When I sold my mental health business and had the freedom to relocate, it was a no-brainer. My wife and I had fallen in love with Central Bucks County and, specifically, wanted to move nine miles up the road to the New Hope area.

That area is as strikingly beautiful, charming, and historic as any place in America. The same considerations that attracted the now famous group of New Hope Impressionist artists over one hundred years ago are still present today. The mists and moods of the Delaware River continually shift as its waters flow by our shores. The hills and dales along the river's bank remain largely open, untamed, and minimally developed with an abundance of 200-plus-year-old stone structures dotting the landscape.

This bucolic setting lies just fifteen minutes from Route I-95 with N.Y.C. just ninety minutes away and Philadelphia sitting fifty minutes to the south. The shops in Flemington, New Jersey, are just fifteen minutes east and the refinement and charm of Doylestown, the County Seat, can be found fifteen minutes to the west.

But the most significant consideration in this discussion is the nature of the New Hope residents. The people are the critical threads that are woven into the fabric of the community. Our fabric is beautiful and is characterized by its diversity and accompanying respect for fellow residents and visitors. This becomes evident once you walk our streets, bike or stroll along the Delaware Canal. It is readily apparent when one visits our galleries, shops, bars and restaurants. Just stop for coffee, or a refreshment of choice, and you will usually find a friendly person sitting nearby who will smile, make eye contact, and engage you in discussion.

If you value freedom of artistic, political, and lifestyle expression, come to New Hope. It is a great place to live and to visit. Even more than that, the New Hope experience engenders a state of being that is transportable. Please come and become part of the New Hope experience.

(Dr. Howard Savin is a psychologist and author. He has a counseling practice in Buckingham, PA.)

All You Need Is Hope

By John Hensel,
"Suburban Gypsy"

When I first moved to New Hope, Pennsylvania, in late 2003, I worked as a waiter at the Lambertville Station restaurant commonly known as "The Station" and later as a trainman on the New Hope & Ivyland Railroad. The job at the railroad entailed absorbing the history of Bucks County, especially New Hope. While reviewing information on the area, I became intrigued by Benjamin Parry, who, in 1790, rebuilt his burned-out business along the river, thus resurrecting his dream and the jobs of many. The "New Hope Mill" was built on the ashes of what had been there before. The words stuck and so did the name of the town where we now live.

New Hope has a very special meaning to me. Once you hear my story, you will understand that I am a person who has come a long way through life and I will not allow stumbling blocks to deter me or slow me down. When my son, Daniel, and I arrived, we had $300 and a few clothes to our name. Maybe fate or providence guided us back here as I had originally left the area in 1969. I really cannot say.

Growing up down the road in Ewing, New Jersey, I already had a loving impression of the area, as my parents and I often wandered the roads throughout the countryside, taking in the old Quaker farmsteads, the barge rides, the great food, and, of course, the flea market. In the lazy summer nights of 1967 and 1968, I witnessed the spirit of the area soar through the many concerts at the nearby Lambertville Music Circus.

At that time, many in my generation became restless with an itch and a yearning to see the world. I was no different and pushed myself out of the nest and into a "new" world, to experience it firsthand. School in Miami led to an interesting career of concert production and in the mid-1970s, I relocated to New York City and lived near the Village—in Soho. There I visited a renowned psychic who shared a vision of me living in California, adapting to a new lifestyle. Three months later, I was on a plane to L.A., to begin a new chapter of my life.

Destiny has always been one step ahead of me. As I sank deeper into the decadence and craziness of Los Angeles, friends appeared out of nowhere—friends from Ewing who had also left the East Coast. They came to pursue the beach life in San Diego, which included heavy doses of ocean, girls, suntans, beer, and work (only when they had to). In late 1979, I moved south to the beach, once again hitting the road. With just a car, a girlfriend, and lots of hope, I had the angels watching over me.

That move was a big step toward my life as it is today. San Diego proved to be an experience that created today's destiny. Years of living at the beach in a lazy town quite like New Hope ended in 1984 as I found my true love, started a business, and became a parent almost overnight.

On a peaceful Christmas Eve in 1989, Daniel was born. Watching him in his crib as a baby, I vowed always to be there for him and to do whatever I could to help him. In 2001, this promise was painstakingly put to the test as my wife, Wendy, passed away from a long illness. My sadness was tempered by my desire to help Daniel become a man, and so we left the death in the West to begin life anew. New Hope (or anywhere else) did not become part of the picture until a few years later when I had a burning desire to find us a "home." Thoughts of the great times from my youth kept coming into my mind during a two-year sales job in Canada. My sights became set on the area where it all began! Again friends (angels) appeared.

In October 2003, Paul, my best friend from high school and college, came forward and guided Daniel and me into New Hope, where another old friend was also living. When we drove into town, Alan Rosenberg remembered when we met in Miami during college. All he had to his name was a broken-down car, so, for a short time, he became a roommate. Cosmic dividends came full circle when Daniel and I rented our first home in New Hope from him at 150 South Main Street. New Hope became a safe place where I could raise a boy in this world.

Working six to seven days a week is scary when you are responsible for a young person. But a funny thing happened along the way. People started caring. Friends, neighbors—even strangers—would ask how things were going. Many would comment on Daniel and discuss whom he was hanging with or his whereabouts. A friendly community involvement began that did not revolve around gossip or nosiness, but a sincere effort of care and support. Walking over the bridge late at night to our little South Main home gave me daily assurance and the confidence that somehow, some way everything would be okay. In 2008, I decided to work in New Hope full time. It's nice to stay close to home. Both Daniel and I still play, work, and live here, and I hope we can stay for a very long time. To all my friends here …THANKS!

Embraceable You

By Matthew Casey

Hope had laid the brick to stem the water's tide.
This town was built by dreamers from a day gone by,
Where artists painted life and poets took the stage.
Together here our story starts a brand new page.

Beautiful Friend,
I hear you calling me again.
In this crazy world I've found one truth,
Keeps me coming back to you,
My Embraceable You.

A town became its name for all to see.
The faces change; it still remains a place for me.
It calls to all you dreamers to come outside.
Togetherness is all we need, so do not hide.

Beautiful Friend,
I hear you calling me again.
In this crazy world I've found one truth,
Keeps me coming back to you,
My Embraceable You.

Year after year the River lashes,
But you don't give up control.

You are more than bricks and mortar.
You are the Hope that's in our Souls.

Daylight shines to show this special place.
We represent the beauty of the human race.
Take my hand and we'll walk here side by side.
We will show the world that Hope is still alive.

Beautiful Friend,
I hear you calling me again.
In this crazy world I've found one truth,
Keeps me coming back to you,
My Embraceable You,
My Embraceable You,
My Embraceable You.

© 2008 by Matthew Casey

(Songwriter Matt Casey resides in Bucks County, PA. He has achieved a number of awards, including a VH1 Honorable Mention 2008, for "Embraceable You" — a song written specifically for New Hope and Up River Production's Embraceable You Project.)

An Ideal Town

By Jen Miller

During my younger years, my parents moved around a lot and I was always feeling somewhat displaced. In 1984, our family finally settled down in one location—Doylestown, Pennsylvania. I was one happy nine-year-old kid.

Even though we lived quite close to New Hope, I really did not discover the town until I was out of college. During the majority of my high school years, plus some of my college summers, I was busy working in Peddler's Village—a charming little complex of specialty shops and restaurants located in Lahaska (which is just a short distance from New Hope).

When I finally discovered New Hope for myself, it was a wonderful surprise. I fell in love with the quaint shops, the fabulous restaurants, and the gorgeous natural scenic beauty. As an adult, I realize how extremely lucky I am to have grown up in such a historically and culturally rich area as Bucks County. It truly is a little "nugget" nestled into the southeastern part of our state.

In grade school, we all learned about the Revolutionary War and George Washington's famous crossing of the Delaware River on Christmas Day, but how many people can hop in their car, travel just a few miles, and find themselves in the exact spot where this historic event actually happened? We are very fortunate to be living in a place that is the cornerstone of our early American history.

New Hope is a small American town that has certainly fulfilled the dreams of our forefathers. This place embodies the belief that "all men are created equal." The richness, diversity, and welcoming attitude of New Hope make it so much more than just a scenic town on the Delaware. To me, it is the embodiment of our American ideals.

I have many wonderful memories of New Hope, but there is one in particular that stands out in my mind. One day I opened up my mail to find a letter informing me that one of my original poems had been accepted for publication. I was absolutely over the moon! I was ready to celebrate. I called my older brother, Rob, and my dear friend, Liana, and the three of us went off to Havana's, one of my favorite places in New Hope. The weather was lousy; it was raining all night—but guess what? The place was packed. It was a great evening from beginning to end. I remember thinking to myself, "It doesn't matter if it pours all night; I have my own sunshine with me."

From the first time that I discovered this wonderful little town, New Hope has remained a bright spot in my life.

I'm Happy, Mom...Believe Me

By Frank DeLuca

When I was eighteen-years-old and living in Feasterville, Pennsylvania, with my parents and five brothers, I enlisted in the service. The year was 1976, and I wanted nothing more than to be a Military Police Officer. Being only five-foot, seven inches, I was a couple of inches too short for the required height of five-foot, nine inches. I remember my army recruiter, Sergeant Dan, telling me to stand tall and try to stretch myself when they measured my height. Well, obviously, that idea did not work, but then I was asked to take the written test anyway. After learning my score, they persuaded me to go into Military Intelligence, and I became an intelligence analyst—a 96 Bravo. Although I wouldn't be a MP, it seemed to be the next best thing. At least I could claim that I was Army Intelligence.

After I had completed my basic training at Fort Leonard in Wood, Missouri, I came home for Christmas and presented my girlfriend, Carol, an engagement ring. At the time, I confused being homesick with being in love. Carol and I married that following June. In December 1977, I wanted to take leave so I could come home and see my new bride. The two of us spent the Christmas holidays together staying at her parent's home in Feasterville. One night Carol and I decided to do something a little "adventurous." We arranged to have a double date with my gay, older brother Billy and his boyfriend Jack. We followed the two of them to a place in New Hope called The Old Cartwheel Inn. The Cartwheel was a bar and a restaurant, as well as a hot dancing spot for both gay and straight folks. Carol and I arrived early and we sat down together while Billy and Jack mingled with the crowd. My brother seemed to know many of the male patrons. I think I may have even been a little jealous of his popularity at the time.

During those years, I was in complete denial of who I was in terms of my sexual identity. There I was, out for a night of fun with my wife. Then a stranger sat next to me and for the next hour his leg leaned against mine. The bar was uncrowded, and yet I never moved my bar stool away. I clearly recall how much I enjoyed sitting next to another man. I now get it. I was being "cruised." At the time, I had no idea of what was really going on. Most so-called straight men would have gotten up or moved closer to their wife or girlfriend, but not me. It wasn't until Carol finally suggested we go elsewhere that I moved. My last thought leaving the Cartwheel was wishing I had come alone.

My next stop was Fort Hood, Texas. Carol was still living with her parents until she finished her studies at Beaver College. After she graduated I moved her down to Texas with me, and we lived together in Killeen for six months. Before I knew it, our marriage was on the rocks. Carol had met another soldier and was ready to make a quick break. When I came back from a week in field training, all the living room wall hangings were missing. It was then I realized Carol had moved out, left me, and soon filed for divorce.

My last six months at Fort Hood were the best times of my life. My friend Reggie, who I had met in basic training, took me out to a couple of gay clubs called "The Austin Country" and "The Private Cellar." I could hardly wait for the weekends. I didn't care if I had to drive two hours to get to Austin—it was worth it. I was having such a great time that I really wanted to stay in Texas, but ultimately, I decided to come back home because I didn't want to be so far away from my family and my home state of Pennsylvania.

After my tour of duty ended in October of 1979, I moved back home to be with my family. Every Friday and Saturday night, my brother Billy and I would go to New Hope to hang out with the boys at another gay club in New Hope called the Prelude. I met my first boyfriend there, Bobby, who was one of the bartenders. When Bobby and I started going together, I made every excuse in the world to get away from home and take a trip to New Hope. My mother started to wonder what was going on. I told her I was visiting my new girlfriend. I even gave her a fictitious name, "Mona." They say that mothers always know, but I wasn't ready to come out yet knowing that mom was still wrestling with trying to accept the fact that Billy was gay. I later learned that she had even written a letter to "Dear Abby" questioning what makes people gay. I was afraid that if I told my mother she would somehow blame herself.

It wasn't until her fiftieth birthday that I found enough courage to come out to her and introduce her to Bobby. I clearly remember the night of her birthday celebration. Mom was so excited about going out to dinner because my father rarely took her out to a fancy restaurant. As we were driving along on our way to the restaurant, I turned to her in the car and said, "Mom, we're not only celebrating your 'Big 5-0' tonight...we're celebrating something else as well." She smiled and then said something like this, "Okay, Frankie, I bet you're going to tell me I have another daughter-in-law" (she was referring to Bobby). We all laughed. Mom took it well, and has since accepted her gay sons. Her feelings are "as long as my children are happy, I'm happy." What a great attitude.

In October of 1980, Bobby and I moved to a townhouse in Village Two. A friend of Bobby's saw an ad in *The Intelligencer* newspaper for a police officer job in New Hope. I was definitely interested. I applied for the job, took the test (my military experience warranted ten extra points to my test results) and I was hired. On July 13, 1981 a lifelong dream of mine was fulfilled. I became a police officer and not just anywhere, but in New Hope!

On my nights off, I worked as a bouncer at the Prelude. I would park behind The Raven and then sprint up to the Prelude so none of the New Hope cops would see me going into a gay bar. One night another bouncer, by the name of Big Larry, and I had to remove a straight guy from the bar for being too aggressive with some women patrons. As Big Larry and I tried to escort him out of the place, his left arm broke free from Larry and he proceeded to give me a good punch in the jaw. We didn't call the police; we decided to just throw him out of the bar. He then rounded up about five of his friends and they waited outside the bar for the two of us to make our exit. I just had a feeling there was going to be trouble that night so I asked about twenty-five other gay guys in the bar to hang around outside after we closed up the place. All I can tell ya is that when that group of five straight, redneck boys saw all twenty-five of us fellas they thought it was best just to hit the road! It's good to have friends.

In February 1988, on one of the coldest days of winter, I had the good fortune of meeting my lifelong partner, Rey. We met by chance at a surprise birthday party for a mutual friend of ours that was being held at the Yellow Brick Toad Restaurant in Lambertville, New Jersey. Rey had a crew cut and wore a bow tie. I will never forget that night. Rey was wearing blue contacts, hiding the fact he had dark brown eyes. I gave him my phone number and he called me a week or so later. Twenty years later, I still like to tease Rey about that evening. I tell him he reminded me of Patrick Duffy when he played "Aquaman" on a 1980s television series.

Rey and I lived in Upper Makefield on Windy Bush Road for seven years. In December 1996, we bought our current home here in New Hope. Rey is now serving his second term on the borough council. I have been with the police department going on twenty-eight years and I look forward to retiring when the time is right. There is no way Rey and I would ever think of moving away from New Hope because we enjoy the community and the people here so much.

I moved my mother and father here in 2007, but unfortunately, my father passed away just six days after they moved into New Hope Manor. My mother misses my dad very much, but she loves New Hope and has made so many wonderful new friends. She loves going to different events in town and last year she was even in the Gay Pride Parade with me. I drove the police car, with mom sitting by my side. Leading the parade was Governor Ed Rendell. My mother can't wait for this year's parade.

To summarize, let me just say I have had an interesting journey to self-discovery. It has been an exciting ride full of many different unexpected twists and turns. My only regret is that I didn't start a diary thirty years ago. There is so much to tell. But, at this point, the only thing worth recording is that I finally got here. I found the real "me." What could be better than living "happily ever after" in a town I love called New Hope.

My New Life

By Marie DeLuca

My name is Marie Rose DeLuca. I have been a resident of New Hope for eighteen months. I was born, raised, and married in Philadelphia, Pennsylvania. My late husband, William John DeLuca, Sr., and I were married in June of 1953. A couple of years later, we moved to Bucks County and bought a brand new split-level house in Feasterville. After living there for over half a century and raising six sons, we eventually moved to New Hope. Our fifth son, Jackie, bought our former home.

All of our six sons (Billy, Frankie, Mark, Richard, Jackie, and Jeffrey) graduated from Neshaminy High School in Langhorne, Pennsylvania. Our second son, Corporal Frank DeLuca, serves with the New Hope Police Department. While serving in the line of duty, he had the opportunity to visit the New Hope Manor for various reasons. Knowing that my husband and I were getting up in years and that we were both having health problems, Frankie thought this would be a great place for us to live. He wanted to bring us to New Hope so that he could better care for us. With the help of all my kids, my husband and I relocated to a new place in New Hope Manor. My boys were all so happy about our move because they do not live very far away. They all live within thirty minutes from us. Sadly, my husband passed away peacefully in his sleep, after having been here for only six days.

I love it here. Everyone in New Hope is so nice and friendly. They make me feel very special. The Manor is only for seniors of fifty-five years of age and over. It is not an assisted living facility. Most of the residents are widows. We have a few widowers and a few married couples. Everyone can decorate the outside of his or her entranceway. When I look around, I think it looks so pretty. On the second Wednesday of every month, we have a "pot luck" get-together. A "social night" is scheduled for the last Saturday of every month. Everyone brings something on both nights. We go on shopping tours by bus, and we have many special events at New Hope Manor.

There are so many places to go to in this town such as art galleries, antique stores, specialty shops, and many fine restaurants. We have two supermarkets—Giant and Super Fresh. There is a CVS pharmacy located behind New Hope Manor just off West Bridge Street. Pharmacists Lee and Christine are very helpful. They call to remind you that a prescription is soon due and they will call you with a reminder to pick up your prescription when it is ready. This is very important to me as I am on many medications. I am thankful that my son, Frankie, picks them up for me since I am not able to walk very far, nor do I drive.

We also have the Bucks County Playhouse here, and I have been to many of the shows. I just love the musicals and look forward to the new season.

My other sons visit me often and take me to lunch or dinner at many of the local restaurants. The Raven is my favorite. My son Frankie and I love to go there so we can listen to Russell Eiffert play the piano. I am the president of the Russell Eiffert fan club. When we leave the lobby of New Hope Manor, Frankie and I always tell people that we are on our way to choir practice!

At the New Hope Celebrates parade last May, I sat in the police car waving to everyone as Frankie drove. Having Governor Rendell leading the parade was such an honor. I had so much fun and felt so loved by everyone who waved back saying, "Hi, Mama DeLuca!" as many of my sons' friends call me. I will be back again this year with United States Congressman Patrick Murphy leading the parade. I just love New Hope and all the people here, and now you know why.

New Hope's Hopes

By Lucianne DiLeo

Dreams of Hope
Themes of Hope
Schemes of Hope

Lots of Hope
Spots of Hope

Glimmers of Hope
Slivers of Hope
Givers of Hope

Little Hope
Some Hope
Big Hope
Great Hope

Our Hope
Their Hope
Your Hope
My Hope

First Hope
Last Hope
Present Hope
Past Hope
High Hope
Special Hope
Future Hope…

…NEW HOPE

Just Like Paradise

By Dorothy Grider

On New Year's Day, 1950, a small Peugeot brought me to New Hope, Pennsylvania, for the first time. In the car were three happy people and an excited black poodle who knew he was going home. As we crossed the bridge from New Jersey, the small town looked like a Christmas card covered with specks of glittery snow.

Just a few days before in New York City, Rhea Talley from the *Louisville Courier Journal*, had interviewed me. She had told me about a man named Jacques Simpson, a fashion photographer from Paris. Jacques lived part-time in New York City and also owned a home in Bucks County. Jacques was hosting a Christmas party in the city, and Rhea asked if I would go with her. I could never turn down an invitation to a party, so of course I responded with an enthusiastic, "Yes!"

It was a festive night. I met many interesting people and enjoyed mingling with the happy crowd. During the evening, I got to talking with Jacques, and he asked if I did portraits. My answer was another enthusiastic, "Yes!" The very next day Jacques came to visit me in my Gramercy Park studio so that he could view my artwork. Right then and there, he commissioned me to paint his portrait. So now, my dear reader, you know why we had come to New Hope...Jacques, Rhea, "Chiffon" (the happy poodle), and me. This was my first visit to Bucks County, and I was about to begin a grand portrait. I was elated.

Each weekend we drove to New Hope, and I continued to create the big portrait that included Jacques, his house on South Sugan Road, and, of course, Chiffon, his beloved companion. Jacques introduced me to his friends, as well as, to many other artists. Occasionally, on a

Sunday night we would go to the Bucks County Playhouse to see a dress rehearsal, as Jacques's friend was the director.

In the early summer of that year, I decided to go to Europe for a short visit and guess what? I ended up staying for seven months. During my European tour, I visited eleven countries and had the privilege of studying painting at the Académie de la Grande Chaumière—one of the most famous art schools in Paris. As much as I loved Paris, eventually I realized it was time to go home. I made the transatlantic trip traveling on the ship *La France* and arrived back in the States in 1951. Jacques was there to meet me.

That same night, Jacques drove me straight from New York to New Hope. Once again, there were three of us packed into the car. This time a young woman named Lydia Gudemann was coming with us. Lydia worked in New York City, but her father lived in New Hope. Lydia and I struck up an instant friendship. The next thing you know, Lydia's father was lobbying me to move to New Hope. He suggested building a studio onto their house. Now that was an offer I couldn't refuse! I designed it, and we found a builder. By 1952, I had moved upstairs to the house on North Main Street in New Hope. I loved living in this little white bungalow overlooking the Delaware…it was just beautiful. Lydia also decided to leave New York City and got a job at the Pidcock Insurance Agency in New Hope. She and her father lived in the downstairs portion of the house.

For several years, this charming little house with its riverside view was the perfect place for me to wile away my days painting and illustrating. However, in 1955, the peaceful atmosphere that we so enjoyed abruptly changed to chaos, loss, and mass destruction. Hurricane Diane, which followed right on the heels of Hurricane Connie, hit the area with an absolute vengeance.

New Hope, called "the little jewel of Bucks County," was completely submerged in water. The town's mayor had issued an evacuation order. He sent a boat down to rescue Lydia, her father, and Annie, their dog, so that they could get out before the storm's ravaging waters started to become deadly. Jacques offered them a safe place to stay at his home on the outskirts of town. I was fortunate to be out of the area when the storm hit as I was down in Kentucky visiting my parents. I managed to make my way back to Bucks County and also took refuge at Jacques's house.

The rains pounded down. The streets became rivers. The bridges were washed out. Hurricane Diane caused hundreds of millions of dollars worth of damage to the Delaware Valley. More than a hundred people in the area lost their lives. Even to this day, Diane is still recognized as the greatest and most devastating flood the Delaware has ever experienced.

When we were able to go back home, we faced the massive task of cleaning up the house. Luckily, my art studio, which was located upstairs in the house, was spared, but the rest of the place was a disaster. Waterlogged rugs and furniture had to be thrown out. Appliances were ruined. We lost all the floors; they were totally warped. The odor of mud was everywhere. Lydia and I would work until 2:00 AM trying to wash away the muddy filth and debris. Those were difficult days. I will always be thankful for the Red Cross volunteers who came to our aid, bringing us food, drinking water, and clean-up supplies. I also remember the convoys of Amish families who just showed up in the area to offer us their assistance. It was a time when everyone pulled together to offer one another comfort, solace, and help.

After the devastating flood, Main Street was repaved. Curbs, driveway entrances, and sidewalks were also added. I had a mailbox at the New Hope post office, which, at the time, was conveniently located downtown. I would go out twice a day for a walk—once to pick up my mail and then again just for the sake of exercising. New Hope was a close-knit community. We knew everybody on the street. Faye and Ben Badura lived across from us. Abbott's had a newsstand and eating-place on South Main Street. Abbott's was one of the local mom-and-pop businesses in town. Men liked to stop by early in the morning for a ten-cent cup of coffee. The place would be buzzing with town gossip and clouds of cigarette smoke at 7:00 AM. In the afternoon, Abbott's was filled with teenagers sipping cherry cokes at the U-shaped counter while sitting on those little round stools that were screwed into the floor. The kids would play the pinball machines and try to sneak a peek at the *Playboy* magazines that were stacked up on the large, wooden magazine rack. We would often gather there for sandwiches or ice cream.

Farther down the street there was a small farmer's market-type of grocery store. This was located at the corner where Farley's Bookshop now stands. It was stocked with fresh local produce. Every morning I would run into Paul Whiteman, the "King of Jazz," who never failed to stop by this neighborhood place to pick up his daily newspaper.

Quite frequently, I had to travel to New York City to take care of my artwork business. I always loved the first leg of that trip that began with a walk over the bridge to Lambertville Station and then a hop on board the little one-coach train called the Toonerville Trolley. The trolley ran on the railroad tracks from Lambertville to Trenton. Whenever I rode that train, I knew I would see the same group of people. I got to know some great friends and traveling companions. In the cold months, there was a potbelly wood stove on board and at Christmas, they put up a tree. The "regulars" on board would even exchange Christmas gifts. There's no doubt about it, the Toonerville Trolley was both convenient and fun.

Living in New Hope was always filled with excitement and surprise. You never knew whom you might spot meandering through the town. Some of the biggest names in show business have performed at the Bucks County Playhouse—Grace Kelly, Helen Hayes, Kitty Carlisle, Lillian Gish, Colleen Dewhurst, Bob Fosse, Robert Redford, Merv Griffin, George C. Scott, and John Travolta—just to name a few. It would not be unusual to find yourself sitting next to a celebrity or a superstar at one of our local restaurants. I remember seeing Liza Minelli riding her bicycle through town. One night we happened to meet Sloan Simpson at a cocktail party. Sloan was the young Texas beauty who in 1949 married Bill O'Dwyer, the mayor of New York City, who was old enough to be her father. By the time we met her, she had long since divorced the mayor and was enjoying a whirlwind life on her own. It was easy to understand why Sloan had earned the reputation as "the Society Queen who enchanted New York." We found her to be exuberant and charming. As we were chatting with Sloan that evening, she mentioned to us that she would like to live in New Hope. We told her the house next door was for sale. Without any hesitation, Sloan bought the house, and it became a gathering place for luminaries and celebrities.

New Hope has been my home for close to six decades. From my studio on the river, I have illustrated about one hundred children's books, five of which I wrote. I have never ceased to be inspired by the resplendent countryside of Bucks County. My walls are covered with oil paintings and watercolors depicting many different beautiful and graceful scenes of New Hope.

I will never forget a visit I had years ago from one of the editors at Rand McNally. It was a lovely afternoon, and the two of us were sitting out on my patio, which, of course, overlooks the banks of the Delaware River. As we sat there together soaking up the tranquil atmosphere, this woman turned to me and said, "Dorothy, I hope you know you live in paradise."

Remembering the Coffee Houses

By Jon Case

Today I would describe my parents as having been bohemians. However, back in the 1950s I did not think of them that way. As an eight-year-old, I thought bohemians were anti-establishment folks, who lived in Greenwich Village, wore berets and black turtlenecks, and spent their angst-filled time in smoky coffee houses reading gloomy, non-rhyming poetry. The fact that my father regularly wore a beret and that he and my mother spent hours in smoke-filled New Hope coffee houses espousing unconventional ideas indicates how clueless I was at that age. Even so, the foggy remembrances of this clueless young boy evoke some sweet, if not reliably factual, memories.

Our family lived in Lambertville, New Jersey, but eschewing their lock-minded community, my parents' social life was centered in New Hope, among its arty and eccentric inhabitants of the time. On almost every clear, warm day, Millie and Elmer engaged in a ritual they began in the early 1940s. They walked across the bridge that connects these two small river towns and spent the middle of the afternoon in coffee houses sipping java and chatting with any number of friends who also took time off to enjoy the day. Perhaps it was not a café society, but certainly a café community.

Very often, when I became old enough, I went along with them on their customary excursions of delightful diversion. The first of these coffee shops that I remember was Helen Louise Cooper's The Snack Shop located at 22 South Main Street. Back in the early 1950s, the building was half its present size with an awning-covered terrace against the south wall enclosed with a white picket fence. The tables and chairs were typical spring-wire metal ice cream parlor pieces. I can still recall the distinct aroma of hamburgers being cooked on the grill, and the sugary sweet essence of long ago spilled Cokes that had been absorbed into the daily mopped flagstone patio. Occasionally familiar friends would stop by and join the group for coffee and conversation. I clearly remember the disconcerting scarecrow-like Tom Kanally. He had a wooden leg that he would paint bright green for St. Patrick's Day. Tom fastened a sock to his peg leg by using a bunch of tacks. Then there was grandfatherly Harry Rosen, a disheveled master sculptor with an always-unshaven smiling face, who eagerly had a funny joke or a silly pun to share.

Fred and Millie MacKenzie had a coffee shop on East Mechanic Street, whose rear windows overlooked the Buck County Playhouse and the millpond. The interior was dim and wood-paneled, always filled with the smell of aromatic, freshly brewed coffee. The floors were the pervasive "pumpkin pine" wide boards typically found in Bucks County buildings, and the tables, chairs, and booths were of old soft wood that had a smooth patina from years of being rubbed by hands, cloths, and bottoms. Millie MacKenzie was an earth-mother angel with twinkling Santa-like eyes and an abundant head of brown hair she wore in a thick braid down her back. She always lovingly treated me as one of the adults, which was a welcome change from the dismissive attitude I often encountered at The Snack Shop. I would sit and listen in wonder to the adult chatter, unknowingly absorbing the humor, acceptance, open-mindedness, and intelligence of these gentle freethinkers and their equally kind friends and patrons.

Like the owners of many coffee shops that came before and those to come after, the MacKenzies soon tired of the long hours and the little profits. Their dream of having a place for locals to gather and enjoy each other's company was worn to a nub. The Coffee House on Mechanic Street closed. Not to worry. It is a universal dream; new coffee shops blossomed. Across from The Coffee House at the intersection of Main and Mechanic Streets, Michael and Peggy Lewis ran their art and furniture showroom called Charles Fourth Gallery. The building had a side yard spread with white gravel. In this space, the Lewis's set up some reclaimed tables, chairs, and coffee makers. In no time at all, the locals gravitated to the Lewis's new impromptu café.

New Hope had become an artist's colony by the late 1940s and early 1950s. This little town in Bucks County had become a rural version of New York's Greenwich Village. Painters, writers, sculptors, furniture designers, antique dealers, shop owners, bohemians, and eccentrics of every stripe were drawn to the beauty, location, and social freedoms of this tiny borough. Not far away in the Doylestown area, the homes of such immensely talented people as Oscar Hammerstein II, Moss Hart, Dorothy Parker, Pearl Buck, and James Michener were located. At Mike and Peggy's on any given sunny day, one could run into local or visiting artists such as Bill Ney, Harry Rosen, Ben Badura, Ranulph Bye, Charles Evans, John Charry, Selma Burke, Budd Schulberg, Patricia Highsmith, George Nakashima, Val D'Ogries, Paul Evans, Phil Powell, Bob Whitley, or Odette Myrtil.

It was at the coffee house tables where these people gathered that I was exposed to the wonder and spirit of brilliant and irreverently creative minds. The boy was losing his naiveté. Silently sitting among these men and women, my brain soaked up this verbal feast like water to a sponge. These talented artists and independent characters discussed art, life, love, and gossiped in a salon-like atmosphere. Race, color, age, finances, sexuality did not define these people—those attributes were accepted as mere characteristics, not definers. Any mention of those personal characteristics was woven into their dialogues, conversations, and jokes naturally and unabashedly. They were rich, poor, destitute, humble, pompous, comic, curmudgeonly, young, old, gay, and straight beings in the same earthly boat. Listening to them, I came to believe that creativity and appreciation of diversity were intrinsically human beings' second natures. These souls cared passionately about the living of life and the richness of its tapestry. I would hear them saying to one another, "Make me laugh!" "Make me think." "Listen to this idea!" "What do you think of that idea?"

In 1955, Elmer bought his first automobile, a bright red 1949 MG-TC two-seater sports car. We no longer had to always walk across the bridge. Whenever our family of five (mother, father, two brothers, and me) would arrive on the scene it was like a circus act. My father would park the car, get out, walk around, and open the passenger door to lift my youngest brother off my mother's lap. Then she would swing her legs out and appear. Next, my older brother and I would emerge, one by one, from the small boot located behind the two seats. People would stare with their mouths agape at this funny car that looked as if it could barely hold two people—let alone five! Secretly I loved the performance and the attention.

Mike and Peggy's coffee shop added a makeshift enclosure that became a kitchen. Soon an overhead canopy was added so that customers could gather on rainy days. But the owners wearied of the relentless work of running two businesses. To the rescue came a new owner, Mel Refuge, who added substantially to the physical facilities and opened Mel's Coffee Shop. With his usual casual panache, he enclosed the terrace, bricked its floor, added a wood stove, and filled the place with artwork. He was now in business year-round in his uniquely decorated second-hand-styled sidewalk café, serving customers breakfasts and lunches. Throughout the 1960s and half of the '70s the famous Mel's thrived. In 1975, Bernard Robin and John Byers turned Mel's into The Apple restaurant. John and I partnered in designing and renovating the funky coffee shop into an Art Nouveau corner bistro. Completing some sort of cosmic circle, Elmer built the sixteen Art Nouveau French doors that became the elegant façade for the new restaurant.

As Mel's thrived on one side of Mechanic Street, another open-air coffee shop/restaurant debuted and succeeded across the street. Howie and Linda Euble opened Number 9. The banked basement of the old house at 9 Mechanic Street was converted into a kitchen, and the rear yard of the property that sloped down to the millpond became the dining area. Artists Court Butterfield and Tony Autorino, jeweler Lou Pace, designer Phil Powell, painters Joe Crilley and Harry Haenigsen, and local characters Dottie House and Bobby Dager were just some of the people who could be found there enjoying summer afternoon camaraderie, sipping coffee, and conversing as if time did not exist.

My parents were amused by how often word got back to them that they were considered by many outside their circle to be independently wealthy; believing they chose to live a bohemian life in spite of all their riches. How else could it be explained that they wiled away endless hours, sitting in coffee houses when others had to toil at making a living? This rumor prevailed because Elmer, a self-employed cabinetmaker, and Millie, a part-time bookkeeper, opted to live a relaxed, fun life, rather than a nose-to-the-grindstone existence. My parents never felt the necessity to dispel this myth.

In the mid 1970s, another restaurant, Mother's, at 34 North Main Street, became the new local coffee hangout. The long established ritual of going for an afternoon cup of coffee had now become a morning exercise. Ground zero for the "morning coffee club" was table number nine at Mother's. There you could find Joe Crilley, Elmer and Millie, Daisey Winston, Charles Tiffany, Phil Powell, Jim Martin, Florence and Jack Rosen, and a slew of others whose work days apparently did not start until noon. The conversation and laughter around table nine would grow more rambunctious as the morning unfolded and the sippers' caffeine highs grew to a raucous crescendo.

These are some of my New Hope memories that revolve around the coffee houses I frequented most often with my parents. There were plenty of other popular hangouts in town, too. If the customers gathered around table nine at Mother's were considered the liberal wing of the New Hope coffee drinking community, then the conservative wing would be found at the Golden Pump, a diner type of coffee shop/restaurant located in the first block of South Main Street. If one wanted to find out the latest scuttlebutt on local business or town council matters delivered in a more serious atmosphere, "The Pump" was the place to eavesdrop over your cup of coffee.

All things must change, as New Hope had to change. The quaint little artists' colony of yesteryear has faded and been transformed into a predominantly tourist town. Peering down a side street or wandering through an alley one can still catch a glimpse of some physical remnants that stand as reminders of times gone by. With business growth, changes in popular cultural and a push from the ever-pressing population growth New Hope has lost its post–World War II sophisticated innocence. This is neither good nor bad—it just is. Those eccentric creative minds, for the most part, have moved on, yet the free-thinking attitudes and open, loving values established by those earlier residents and artisans are still the essence of New Hope.

(After attending college in New York City, Jon Case returned to live in the New Hope/Lumberville area from 1970 to 1995 where he had an architectural design/build company. He was the founding president of FACT Bucks County.)

On Being "Mother's"

By Joe Luccaro

My good friend Bobby Blanche, who owns Rice's Flea Market, always introduces me as "Joe Luccaro—you know, the guy who used to own Mother's Restaurant." Yes, that's me. I spent thirteen years at Mother's, from 1976 to 1989. Twenty years later, people still come up to me and tell me how much they miss Mother's Restaurant. "Can't you do it again, Joe?" they always ask. The truth is, it would be pretty impossible.

The 1970s were an exciting time in New Hope. Mother's was a continuation of the local hangout restaurants that had always existed in town. There was the Canal House owned by Johnny Francis; Pamela Minford's Hacienda Restaurant; and Odette's, owned by the former Parisian stage and screen performer Odette Myrtil. These were the most frequented places in town.

Most of the morning regulars that wandered down to Mother's were transplanted patrons from Mel's, a New Hope institution located on the corner of Main and Mechanic Streets. If you stepped into Mother's at any time of the day, there was one table where all the action was—and that was table number nine, the round table in the back room. This table was the epicenter of town gossip and wisdom. Local artists, shop owners, and "characters" spent countless hours drinking coffee and dispensing "advice" from table number nine.

Let's see...there was Jim Martin, Anthony Autorino, Bob Whitley, Mayor Jim Magill, Elmer and Millie Case, Bob Rosenwald, Ray Halacy, Jack Rosen, and Phil Powell—just to name a few. At lunch and dinner the crowd changed. It became an eclectic mix of tourists, old hippies, and newcomers, along with the local restaurant regulars. Our creative staff whipped up all sorts of great salads, sandwiches, dinner specials, and the most decadent desserts in the whole wide world. (In those days, no one had ever heard of a low-carb diet!)

Mother's got its start in 1975 when a local restaurateur, Michael Short, helped us to turn La Casserole at 34 North Main Street into a completely new concept: a restaurant that featured delicious "comfort food," you know, the kind of food that only a mother could make. The staff at Mother's was quite unique. My partner was Stephanie Pomerantz who used to run the kitchen at John and Peter's. She was a real dynamo. We hired feminists, hippies, and drop-outs—the greatest staff you could possibly imagine! In no time at all we became *the* place for breakfast, lunch, and dinner.

Years earlier, my wife Amy and I bought another Michael Short restaurant in Stockton, New Jersey, called Renaissance and renamed it Le Bistro. (The restaurant is still in operation under the name of Villa Ponte.) It was a dinner-only place. On July 4, 1976, Le Bistro was sold. I decided that I wanted to put everything I had into Mother's.

It was a good decision. The business grew. We purchased the building next door. Jim Hamilton did the design and Joe Balderston and others worked on the building. John Brown designed and built the outside garden and sitting areas. These were exciting times.

The staff was rapidly growing. We were fortunate to have an outstanding crew. The kitchen at various times included Martine Landry, who went on to open her own restaurant, Martine's; Jimmy and Jane Faraco, who later opened Havana Bar and Restaurant; Jerry Horan, who is at the Centre Bridge Inn; Jackie Bowe, the former owner/chef of Full Moon restaurant in Lambertville, New Jersey; and current head chef at HollyHedge Estate, José Calderon. All of these incredibly talented people had their start at Mother's and it makes me happy to think we served as the launching pad for their future success.

The front of the house was staffed with the likes of Robert Ebert, who went on to The Raven; Maryanne and Sallie Mahoney, their next stop was Bell's Tavern in Lambertville; Michael Miel, who started Miel's Restaurant in Stockton; and Jimmy Skea—I'm not sure where Jim ended up.

Patrons could rub elbows with the rich and famous. The notables we served included Julia Child, Rod Stewart, Abbie Hoffman, George Nakashima, Jessica Savitch, and Geraldine Ferraro. They all came for the experience: funky atmosphere and great "comfort" food. The most popular items? Breakfast: remember the pheasant and Florentine omelet? Lunch: the George E. Price—a sandwich made of turkey, bacon, and Swiss cheese with Russian dressing poured on top and Chicken Lickin'—a boneless chicken breast served on garlic bread, wrapped with Provolone cheese and topped off with an oyster and sherry sauce.

How about dinner? Veal Mother's—a thin filet of veal, filet mignon, and chicken covered with sliced mushrooms and Marsala cream sauce, and Cajun *anything*. Believe me; we could satisfy your cravings for Creole cooking long before it became part of the national cuisine. Best of all was dessert. On display, as you entered the "Deli", were the most marvelous, mouth-watering creations including mocha amazons, banana hazelnut tortes, and chocolate raspberry gateaux. The trick was to pick out your dessert *first* and then plan the rest of your meal around that initial dessert choice. Our bakers Suzanne, Jeannine, Karen, Gail, and Doug were the absolute best. Everything was made from scratch with only the finest ingredients.

Mother's was the place to be. As I said, it was an exciting time.

(In 1971 Joe and Amy Luccaro honeymooned in the New Hope area, moved there one year later, and have never left. They are the owners of HollyHedge Estate, New Hope, PA.)

There's No Place Like New Hope

By Patricia Cilenti

There is something to be said about a place in the world that reflects your hopes and dreams and sparks your drive and ambition to reach higher. New Hope, Pennsylvania, is just that place. We had lived in Pennsylvania when 9/11 occurred and felt the impact of that devastation and the emotional rush of fear that weighed heavily on our spirits. After a week's spring vacation, we relocated to Virginia Beach, Virginia, where we resided for six years, but never really felt at home.

In the summer of 2008, we finally decided to move back "North" where we sensed we essentially belonged. We had no real destination in mind so we spent the summer traveling to different locations in exploration of a community and a lifestyle that would fit our personal needs, an idea of what a community and home are. The traveling alone was hard enough, forty-five days in all, compounded with three carsick children and a large black Lab riding in a car. Needless to say, we were exhausted from searching New York, Connecticut, New Jersey, and Pennsylvania. We were finding towns that were "like New Hope" and with each trip we stopped in New Hope on the way back to Virginia Beach with the feeling of misspent time and without a positive outcome. At least there was New Hope. And there was the answer we had been searching for: a town that had the essence and quality we wanted. *We should just move to New Hope*!

The first weekend of September we packed our children and all of our things and made the trip for one last time. We arranged for a monthly rental while we searched for a permanent address. The powerful inspiration of New Hope comes through each person you meet here.

Honestly, if you have an idea and you articulate it to some people in town, they will be quick to give you feedback and offer valuable assistance in making your dreams come true.

Within the first two months of living here, I wrote and photographed a children's story called, *"What's That Noise?" A Little Girl's Move to a New Little Town*. It is about our three-year-old daughter and her exploration of the sounds of New Hope, from the waterfall to the train and the horse and carriage. In March 2009, we opened a store, Simply SOTA, at 26 North Main Street, with the same support and inspiration from our wonderful community. My husband also started a new business, based on a dream that he has always had of making a marinara sauce. This product is quickly becoming a popular local favorite.

New Hope is a place where individual preferences, creativity, and styles are respected, not for just one particular circumstance, but as a way of life.

Funky and Fun

By Serena Weil

New Hope is special to me not because of just any old reason. New Hope is historical, it's funky, and it's fun. I moved here in September of 2004 when I was four-years-old.

It is an awesome experience living in New Hope. There are great people, shops, and views. There are many restaurants such as Havana, Starbucks, Dilly's, and more. Another thing is that New Hope is a tourist town. Lots of people like to come here. I can see why. Many hotels such as the Nevermore and the Logan Inn are great places.

It is always fun to walk along the towpath or dip my toes in the cool, fresh Delaware River. If it's a warm, sunny day, my family likes to walk across the pedestrian bridge and see if we can spy Bowman's Tower in the distance. Anyone can come here, learn, and actually walk in the footsteps of George Washington. Also, Bowman's Tower was his lookout during the Revolutionary War. He crossed the ice-filled Delaware River in the middle of the night on Christmas. Someone told me that George Washington once stayed at a private residence in Lambertville, New Jersey, which is a sister-city to New Hope.

New Hope is a great place to live.

Rearranging My Life

By John Byers

"Don't move any shrubs" and "Don't rearrange any furniture!" Those were always the last words my parents shouted to me as my dad backed the car down the driveway of our home in Upper Dublin, Pa. I smiled and waved bye-bye. Even if they were only gone for a couple of hours, I relished the thought of landscaping the garden and transforming the living room.

My parents just didn't get it. They expected their teenage son to hang out with the "right" crowd; study hard and get good grades; participate in team sports; and most of all, not interfere with their way of life. I was happy to comply with the last request.

One day I got a call from my older sister who was living in Doylestown at the time, asking me if I would like to go antiquing in a little village of Bucks County called New Hope. "At least someone in this family gets it," I thought to myself. That first visit to New Hope literally filled me with a sense of hope. As soon as I turned sixteen and got my driver's license, I headed back there as often as possible. At last, I had found a place where I felt like I belonged.

After completing high school, I started the next phase of my education in Philadelphia. This was the late 1960s—the war in Vietnam was raging and the draft was hanging over my head. I was clear about one thing . . . there was no way I was going to Vietnam. As luck would have it, I drew an extremely high lottery number from Uncle Sam. Thankful for my good fortune and breathing a big sigh of relief, I knew this was the time to make a significant change in my life. I dropped all of my studies, walked away from school and left behind my friends and family. I decided to make a new life in New Hope.

Pamela Minford, the statuesque blonde entrepreneur who was nicknamed the "Howard Hughes" of New Hope, hired me to work as a "houseboy" at her luxurious Hacienda Inn. The Inn, located at 36 West Mechanic Street, was small, plush, and a romantic hideaway located right in the heart of town. The rooms and suites all included a mini-fridge stocked with a variety of complimentary snacks and goodies. Okay, I'll admit it…those treats often provided the meal that a struggling, starving, hard-working young houseboy was in need of. I can now say "thanks" to Pam for helping me to survive those beginning months on my own.

My next job in New Hope involved creating a favorable and somewhat deceptive impression. Even though I had not yet turned twenty-one, I interviewed with Johnny Francis for a job at the Canal House. Apparently I displayed such a "grown-up" appearance and demeanor that Johnny never even inquired about my age. The Canal House was always a popular and lively gathering place. I waited tables, served drinks, and actually started making a weekly salary that I could live on. I moved on from the Canal House and got a job at the History House, which was a shop that specialized in custom framing. The shop was located in what is now the Bar Room of Karla's. My favorite hangout was Mel's Coffee House, the open-air café located at the corner of Mechanic and Main Streets. Mel's was packed with beatniks and hippies, actors, writers, artists, and even some regular local chess players. People came here to see and be seen. It was a funky little place—famous for Olde English grilled cheese sandwiches, mismatched hotel silverware, a visiting chicken named "Albertine," and coffee priced at (gasp!) 50 cents a cup. As I joined the locals who congregated there day and night, I knew I was in the center of the town's action. The action picked up for me, personally, when someone introduced me to the property owner of Mel's restaurant. It wasn't long before Bernard Robin and I became friends, lovers, partners, and eventually, business investors.

Using some money that I inherited when my great-aunt died, I took the plunge and made my first real estate investment. For a small down payment, I bought three shabby-looking townhouses in Lambertville, New Jersey. My time had come. Now I could unleash my passion for remodeling, renovating, and designing. I fixed up the first one, got it ready for sale, and then contacted a realtor. "Looking at the comparables, I would say that $18,000 is the fair listing price," she told me. I shook my head, telling her, "No way." I had another "comparable" fixed in my mind. "Listen, I've seen houses in Society Hill that are not as nice as this one and they're selling for $35,000," I told her. She thought I was nuts, but the house was listed for $30,000. It sold for $29,000. That sale marked the start of a profitable new career for me. I continued to make money buying, fixing, and reselling a multitude of properties. The pieces of my life were now getting arranged according to what I loved doing best.

I eventually bought Mel's Coffee Shop and renamed it "The Apple." (At that time there was a big, old apple tree located on the corner near the café.) Our new restaurant sign was shaped like a huge apple. The front of the sign had our name written in bold letters and the reverse side depicted a hunk of the apple that had been cut out and in that empty "bite" were the words "Thank You!" I started the process of applying for a liquor license (Mel did not have one.) I hired a corporate lawyer and, after quite a fight, he was successful in getting us our permit. Needless to say, business was booming after we added alcoholic drinks to the menu.

In the mid-1970s, my restless spirit told me it was time for a change. I left New Hope and headed south to Palm Beach, Florida. It seemed like a hip and trendy place to be. I rented a fabulous place a couple of blocks off Ocean Boulevard. Tropical weather, pristine beaches, great clubs, a rocking nightlife—it was all there. With this relocation, I also decided it was time to explore a new vocation. I bought all the tools and supplies to become a potter. Working with a contractor, I would provide all of the handmade tiles. This new venture was short-lived. It didn't take much to lure me back to New Hope. I kept saying to myself, "Palm Beach is nice, but New Hope is more real."

Once more, I returned to the place that truly felt like "home" to me. I took a job at the Phillips Mill Inn and ended up working there for ten years. I found a historic house in Lumberville right along the river's edge that I bought and fixed up. I met a new partner and together we enjoyed being an active part of the New Hope community.

Although Lumberville offered us a sense of peacefulness and charm, we wanted to get back into the heart of things. I ended up buying a couple of properties located along Fisher's Alley. The location was perfect. We were right in the heart of New Hope and we even had parking.

Throughout all the decades that I spent in New Hope, there was one single thread of constancy for me. I never lost my attraction to old houses. Nothing motivated me more than a new renovation project. I continued to buy properties, negotiate deals, rehab houses, and eventually I got my realtor's license.

In December 2000, I made a purchase that would push my life into a completely new direction. I bought the property at the end of Fisher's Alley, which Carol Reynolds had owned and operated as a bed and breakfast. Carol really did not have her heart in the business. After a couple of years, she was ready to move on. The property was on the market for over a year, but no interested buyers ever appeared. One day Carol approached me (since I was living just a few steps away) and after considerable deliberation and negotiation, we finally made a deal.

"Oh my God, what have I done?" I thought to myself. I sat alone in a bleak-looking room of this newly acquired property and for the first time in my life, I questioned myself. "Is this ever going to work? Is it possible to turn this place around? What's it really going to take to convert this site into a profitable business?" It was clear that there was more work to be done than I ever imagined.

My goal was to open on Valentine's Day. That gave me exactly six weeks to do a complete overhaul to the dining room, the downstairs common room, as well as getting four bedrooms fixed up and ready to rent. I sprung into action . . . stripping and painting, adding paneling and molding, refinishing floors, hanging chandeliers, and filling the place with French and English antiques. On February 14, we welcomed our first guests to the newly remodeled "Porches on the Towpath."

My next big project was to add wraparound porches to both levels of the house. During this phase of the renovation, we warned our guests ahead of time that they would need to walk a "gangplank" in order to get in the front door. No one seemed to mind. In fact, it made the comings and goings a little more exciting!

Porches has provided me with endless opportunities for creating, renovating, designing and decorating. Over the past nine years, I have added all kinds of "finishing touches" to the guest rooms in the main house. I've landscaped the property and designed a whimsical garden filled with classical statues, a sundial, a fishpond, a gazebo, cascading flowers, sheltering trees, shrubs, and bordering hedges. In 2005, I opened up the "Gate Keeper's Cottages" which gave us four more additional rooms to rent. In 2008, I completed a new section of Porches and named these two rooms the "Private Quarters."

Running a bed and breakfast has been a whole new venture for me. One more time I rearranged my life, but this time I discovered how I could make all the pieces fit into one entity.

With Porches, I combined my love of antiques and my passion for renovating and decorating, gardening and landscaping, along with my experiences in the restaurant business and rolled them all into one. Most of all, this business has given me the opportunity to meet so many fascinating people.

A long time ago someone once gave me this piece of advice, "Arrange whatever pieces come your way." That's what I have tried to do throughout my life. New Hope is such a special place. The warmth and ambience of this close-knit community have allowed me to form new patterns with the different pieces of who I am. I have been here for more than four decades. I don't know what the future will bring, but of this much I am certain—no one will ever be able to tell me that I can't move shrubs around and can't rearrange furniture to my heart's content. That, for me, will always be happiness.

(John Byers is the owner/proprietor of Porches on the Towpath Bed & Breakfast. He is alive, well, and living in New Hope.)

An Example of Being Earnest

By Susan Sandor

It was sometime in December when we were making a right turn from our driveway heading for McCarter Theatre to see *The Importance of Being Earnest* staged when we noticed a shimmering red fringe lacing the mouth of our mailbox. In spite of the fact that we were running slightly behind schedule (never, ever, are we late), curiosity compelled me to stop the car and hop out to retrieve a foil bag with a pretty ribbon and an envelope bearing our handwritten names in gold ink. "Rabbit?" I asked myself eyeing the shape and feeling the weight of the packaged contents. That notion was dispelled upon breaking the wax seal and reading the tender missive on the enclosed card from our neighbors.

To paraphrase, the message went something like this: Our zeal for gardening went into overdrive, causing us to purchase thousands of hyacinth bulbs to welcome the spring. After putting over 3,000 in the ground, we gardeners had had enough. Enough of what? Neck aches, backaches, and bulbs. So it was decided that the best thing to do was to send the remaining "little suckers" to gardening friends and to be able to enjoy the fruits of *their* labor in addition to our own. The note was signed "Keith and Filippo."

Next morning I dutifully scouted out the ideal bed for the thoughtful gift of one hundred bulbs. Cupping a tin of fertilizer, a spade, and a rake, one of spring's first harbingers were put into the soil, watered, and mulched. My dear husband, Herbert, who inevitably disappears at the thought of lifting a shovel, suddenly appeared after the project was completed asking where he will be able to stop to smell the hyacinths. But I decided to keep the location a secret and allow Mother Nature to make her grand debut a few months down the road. It would be much more fun to let nature herself point my husband in the right direction. In March, he was surprised to see sprouts pushing through the ground by the lamppost where there were none before, but he was even more surprised to see that the emerging flowers happened to be crocuses, not hyacinths!

I believe our neighbors take our area's true and popular slogan, *Bucks Beautiful*, very, very personally. The message on the accompanying card was printed rather than handwritten so I assume there were many other diggers who were recipients of these bags of joy. I also believe that someone else may have actually gotten hyacinths, but were told that crocuses were in their bag. And that the message on the card was just a story told in earnest in a typically untypical New Hope fashion, provoking smiles in winter and again in spring.

(Susan established Strenk Sandor Advertising in New Hope in 1983 and is working on a book of essays entitled My Mother's Teeth. This article first appeared in the New Hope Gazette in 1999.)

New Hope Shopping

By Denise Zienowicz

Lush green, floral dotted
bricks on bricks,
tiny town,
quietly amused by shoppers
seeking, candles to dream with,
sad songs to sing with,
art galore yet so
much more,
captivating culture
and unwinding whims,
unearthing childlike
mystery from deep
within,
Dark metals, lanterns lit
a stage in time,
each visitor here to find,
quirky as tie-dyed,
that's died and been
born again,
staged a setting
to find peace in
its own breathless hymn.

Crystal Palace Magic

By Lynda Jeffrey Plott

I finished buttoning up my black shirtwaist dress, slipped on the white pinafore apron, and fastened the frilly round doily to the top of my head and . . . *voila!* I was now a Crystal Palace waitress.

During the summer of 1962, I started working for Joe Meo and Joe Wiley who owned the fabulous Crystal Palace Restaurant & Ice Cream Parlor located at 15 Bridge Street (the last building on the right just a few steps away from the start of the sidewalk to the New Hope-Lambertville Bridge). The "two Joes," as they were known throughout the town, had been living in New York City. Joe Meo was a window decorator for Macy's and Joe Wiley was a dancer in the theater. They enjoyed their weekend escapes to New Hope so much, that they finally decided to leave the city. They bought a house near Aquetong Road and immediately wowed the village with their unique ideas and their flair for business.

The Crystal Palace Restaurant was located in the left-hand wing of the Bridge Street building. The "two Joes" had created a lavish, rich, and ornate Victorian atmosphere, one with gingerbread woodwork, vintage light fixtures, and heavy velvet drapes dripping with silk fringe and tied back with elegant swags. The walls were covered with pictures in gilt frames. Leafy green ferns in cloisonné pots were tucked into the corners of the room. An elaborate walnut serving cabinet with drawers and cupboards below served as the "utility station" for all of the basic restaurant necessities: silverware, napkins, water pitchers, and coffee cups. How classy!

I was just fifteen-years-old at the time, and this was my very first job. I believe my mother had lobbied Joe Meo on my behalf. I was absolutely thrilled to be waiting tables in this magical atmosphere, surrounded by a host of other young teenagers. I quickly caught on to the routines and the timing. I learned how to manage the hot-headed cook—don't ask for any substitutes—and I mastered the art of sweet talk with my customers if there was an unusually long wait. "May I offer you something more from our relish tray while you're waiting for the Diamond Jim sandwich?"

A specialty item on the Crystal Palace bill of fare was "Sumptuous Relishes." Customers would help themselves from a three-sectioned dish to a heaping portion of red kidney bean salad, bell peppercorn relish, and a chutney salad. Having such a plain palette myself, these side dishes always struck me as being quite exotic, and yet the customers could not get enough of these "freebie" offerings.

Joe Meo was the master of every situation. He was the epitome of patience and kindness. However, there was one thing that would predictably ruffle his feathers, and that was . . . an empty relish tray. We quickly learned to be Johnny-on-the-spot with keeping those relish trays filled to the brim. After all, nobody wanted to get one of those "hellish-relish" scowls from the boss.

In the nice weather, the Crystal Palace featured outdoor dining. There was a beautiful screened-in veranda, as well as a multitude of riverside tables. People would stream down that narrow little walkway alongside of the building as they headed towards the maitre d' on duty, who was usually Joe Meo. It wasn't uncommon for them to demand that they be given a premier table with a riverside view. Aha! We quickly learned that when you were assigned to tables one to five nearest to the river, you were in for a night of big tips.

Business was booming in the summer. People loved dining outdoors. Besides the ever-popular riverside tables, customers would often request to sit at one of the tables that featured large, overstuffed wicker chairs. They would lounge back in their comfy seats, cool off with a tutti-frutti, and soak in the ambience of a sunny summer day or as night descended, a star-filled sky.

Late in the evening, after the crowds left the Bucks County Playhouse, we could count on a huge surge of business. All of a sudden, the place would be packed. Waitresses would be rushing to take the orders and busboys would be scrambling to turn over the tables. We were always relieved when we could finally say, "Sorry, we're closed," and turn away that last customer.

We had perfected our closing duties with great speed, so that we could finally ... SIT DOWN! I would kick off my Capezio flats, rub my sore feet, empty my heavy pockets of all those jingling coins, and tally up the final earnings for the day. Ten percent for the busboy and all the rest was mine. On a busy weekend, I could brag to all of my friends, "Guess what? I made forty dollars in just two days." Pretty soon, my savings would allow me to stop by the Tony Sarg Shop and splurge on something new.

The ice cream parlor (located on the right-hand wing of the building) was filled with items of nostalgia and magic, as well as a million different sweet temptations. The focal point of the room was the grandiose, wooden-carved soda fountain with a gleaming marble counter and silver taps. The soda fountain was embellished with a large horizontal mirror and stained-glass panels. The decor was sumptuous with paneled walls, a tiled floor, and overhanging polished brass light fixtures with frosted shades. A scattering of old-fashioned parlor tables and chairs filled in the rest of the space surrounding the fountain. The menu was overwhelming . . . fizzy concoctions, malted milkshakes, root beer floats, ice cream sodas and sundaes, and the king of them all—the banana split. Oooooooooo, and if you felt really daring, you might order the house specialty: a "Lillian Russell," which was a half a cantaloupe scooped out and filled with two "buxom" scoops of French vanilla ice cream, topped off with dollops of whipped cream and two maraschino cherries. An order for a "Lillian" invariably caused an outbreak of giggles. Typically, during that day and age, only guys were hired to serve as the soda jerks. (The term "soda jerk" came from the jerking action the server would use on the soda fountain handle when adding the soda.) Most of the high stools in front of the fountain were usually occupied by a flock of young girls who were busy sipping, chatting, and flirting. Not many workers like to return to their place of employment on days off, but the Crystal Palace soda fountain was always my favorite hangout. Perched on that high stool, sipping my cherry coke ever so s-l-o-w-l-y to make it last long enough for Ricky Knoster (my favorite soda jerk) to notice me was my idea of teenage bliss.

The summers passed quickly in those years. After four years, I had evolved from being a nervous, shaky fifteen-year-old waitress to a seasoned old hand who knew all the tricks of the trade. I could empty the ashtrays in a jiffy, fill up the water glasses before they ran dry, and, most importantly, keep those relish trays filled to the brim. After my second year in college, I reluctantly turned in my white organdy apron and said farewell to my two most favorite bosses in the whole wide world. With pleasure, I also handed them back that round lace doily which had flattened down my bouffant "Bubble" hairdo for years. But the happy memories of those magical summers that I spent at the one-and-only Crystal Palace Restaurant in New Hope, Pennsylvania, are mine to keep forever.

(Lynda Jeffrey Plott is a veteran teacher, a freelance writer, and a former teenage waitress extraordinaire.)

A Decade On…
A Decade Off…A Decade On

By Wendy Gladston

I returned to New Hope in December of 2007. Let's just say I had been out of town for a while. My husband and I decided to get back together again after splitting up for a while. I don't know…is twelve years considered "a while"?

We remarried on June 18, 2008. So I have now celebrated my first anniversary of my second marriage, along with the eighteenth anniversary of my first marriage—all to the same man. Not to mention the first date twenty-three years ago. Did you get all that?

New Hope became our home in 1993 after moving from New York City. Like many New Yorkers we had spent a lot of our time getting out of town. Bird watching had become our favorite pastime, and it often took us out of the city and into the country. My husband, Gene, who is a native New Yorker, had spent time tubing on the Delaware River years ago and had always talked fondly of it. So when the time was right, we found ourselves making the big move to New Hope—actually it was to Solebury, but who's counting.

Our house-hunting experience consisted of my coming to the area midweek to narrow down the list to a few homes that Gene would see over the weekend. After deciding against a place in New Jersey, the real estate agent turned to us and said, "You guys belong in New Hope." I don't remember the woman's name, but I never got to thank her. I found the right place on Solebury Mountain and that was it…we never looked back.

As I said earlier, there was a period in my life when I decided to take a twelve-year "hiatus." During those years when I was away, I kept being reminded of New Hope. I am a native of Southern California and so that is where I returned—far, far away from New Hope—or so I thought. But not really. I discovered that people everywhere knew of New Hope. A gay comedian in Long Beach, California, said she used to spend weekends in New Hope. A woman I met in Burbank told me her brother was married to the daughter of the chef who owns the Golden Pheasant on River Road. Even out on the West Coast I was constantly bumping into these little reminders of New Hope. Small world!

I missed the place. Everything kept pointing me back to New Hope. The beauty, the people, and the uniqueness were like nowhere else I had ever been. I was very proud to have lived in New Hope.

After a serendipitous turn of events, I returned to New Hope and into the arms of the love of my life. The time I spent away has honestly faded into something of a dream. I cannot see me not being here, and Gene and me not being together. I believe that New Hope, the place itself, has a lot to do with that feeling. How can a person live happily somewhere else after experiencing New Hope?

One other thing. I have discovered the secret of how to make a good relationship last for over twenty-three years. It's a simple formula. One decade on…one decade off…a decade on…well, you get the idea.

Welcoming Hope

By Reverend Ginny Miles

My family and I moved to Buckingham, Pennsylvania, late in the summer of 1978. Sometime during the first year or two that we were here, we decided to take a day trip to New Hope. I clearly remember how much we enjoyed that day. As we walked along Main Street, which was dotted with many little shops and boutiques, I purchased a pewter butterfly necklace that I still wear. I remember thinking to myself, "What a quaint and pretty town this is!" We thoroughly enjoyed that first visit, and we returned every now and then for subsequent day trips. During those years, we were so busy with our children and other family activities that I did not get back to New Hope as often as I would have liked. But these days it's a much different story.

Almost four years ago, a number of folks in the congregation that I serve as pastor, Penns Park United Methodist Church, believed we were being called to be an "open and affirming" congregation. We believed God was calling us to welcome *all* people to our church regardless of sexual orientation, ethnicity, or race. In particular, we felt a strong desire to reach out to the lesbian, gay, bisexual, and transgender (LGBT) community. We believed we were being called to help heal some of the hurt and pain that has been inflicted through the years on LGBT people and their families by members of many churches. And so my trips to New Hope became more frequent as I sought out ways to meet new people and build relationships. As I walked up and down Main Street and Bridge Street, I began to meet new people. I also began to see the beauty of New Hope in a different way. Perhaps more importantly, I began to appreciate and love New Hope for the uniqueness, creativity, diversity, and the strong sense of community that is so much a part of the town.

God has created us with such different gifts, different talents, and different abilities. I am constantly amazed at God's creativity and in no other place is it more evident than in the LGBT community. Wherever you look, in New Hope and in the LGBT community, you see a gorgeous rainbow of diversity and creativity. It is good!

The LGBT community is in many ways a close-knit community. Unfortunately, the accepting environment of New Hope is not always the norm in all places. This group must stand together against the onslaught of hate and prejudice directed their way much as any family stands together against the difficulties of the world. The LGBT community reminds me a bit of the Delaware River. At times, we can stand at Ferry Street Landing Park and watch as the river flows peacefully along its banks. At other times, the water is rough and sometimes it even overflows its banks. In a similar way, it seems to me that sometimes we go about our daily activities peacefully, doing our own thing, oblivious to the diversity around us. Then at other times we become aware of diversity, but because it is different and unfamiliar, we are afraid to embrace it. Suddenly, it feels as though life is tossing us about. At such times, it is often a very human reaction to hold back and shy away from something we do not know. Sometimes what results is something negative, sometimes ugly.

As a clergy person, I could have been on the receiving end of that same kind of negative reaction myself. I could have been ignored or turned away when I began to try to develop relationships in the LGBT community. I find it ironic that so many folks have been so welcoming to me when the church has been so unwelcoming to them. I will always be so grateful for the warm welcome I have received and for the many friends I have made. The theme for the 2009 New Hope Pride Parade was "Ride the Wave of Diversity." Wouldn't it be wonderful if everyone could learn to ride that wave of diversity? If only we could learn to embrace diversity and to celebrate the differences that make us unique. What a positive difference that would make in our communities!

How boring, how monotonous, how dull, life would be if we were all the same. But God, in God's infinite wisdom, has made us all different. I believe God rejoices in and celebrates our differences. I believe God wants *us* to rejoice in and celebrate our differences. I can just imagine God dancing when we recognize and rejoice in our diversity. Can you?

From the days of the Hebrew Scriptures, we are told to love our neighbor. In the New Testament, Jesus gave his disciples a new commandment to love one another as Jesus has loved and loves us. "Love one another" is the message that we at Penns Park have tried to communicate during our participation in various community activities. You may have noticed that "Love one another" was the message on the banners on our trailer and on the tags on the candy bags we handed out along the New Hope Celebrates parade route.

To me, to love one another means among other things, to respect, accept, celebrate, rejoice, and to work for justice and equality as we celebrate the rich diversity that is found in such abundance in New Hope. I long for the day when diversity will be welcomed, embraced, and celebrated. Let's work together to make that day come soon!

(Reverend Miles feels blessed to be in ministry to and with the LGBT community.)

Our Town

By Matthew Casey

Billy's where you go when you need to get a car
Dave and Ray you know, they have the best bar
If music is the thing you need, we've got every sound

There's Melissa selling ice cream; Sal has got the shirts
There's tourists walkin' round, you can pick out all the flirts
It's easy to see, it's the best around
So tell me, where you can go just to let your hair down
Just to be who you are—it's in Our Town

So, meet me down at Bridge and Main.
We'll walk Our Town together and I'll hold your hand
Take a look around—we are family
Ain't that how it's supposed to be

Let's get down to Martine's, have ourselves a drink
Or sit down by the river; take a little time to think
Havana's where you wanna watch people passing by
Take a visit to the old mill, we can see a play
There's artists in the alley—go hear what they have to say 'cause
Everybody's here they come far and wide
So tell me, where can you go just to let your hair down
Just to be who you are, it's in Our Town

So, meet me down at Bridge and Main.
We'll walk Our Town together and I'll hold your hand
Take a look around—we are family
Ain't that how it's supposed to be

So tell me, where you can go just to let your hair down
Just to be who you are—it's in Our Town

So, meet me down at Bridge and Main
We'll walk Our Town together and I'll hold your hand
Take a look around—we are family.

Yeah, smile because of what we've found
Freedom's what we're feeling when we're in our town
It's why we're here—we are family
Yeah, ain't that how it's supposed to be Our Town.
Yeah, ain't that how it's supposed to be
Our Town.

(Music and lyrics by Matthew Casey. Created for Embraceable You, a New Hope Documentary. www.soundclick.com/matthewcasey.)

Living the Green Dream

By Hope Blaythorne

Living in New Hope is being in touch with nature. It's living along the edge of the Delaware River and watching the eddies and swirls of this magnificent body of water; it's standing at the "wing dam" and listening to the roaring rapids below; it's traveling through the gentle hills and sloping valleys to explore waterfalls, green dells, babbling brooks, and silent springs. The people of New Hope have a deep love and respect for all of the natural wonders of our area.

We do not take this beautiful land of ours for granted. The citizens of this community have worked hard to conserve and protect green spaces and to make sure our natural resources are not being exploited. We have made a conscious effort to teach preservation in all of our actions. So far, we have successfully preserved the largest cold-water limestone spring in the Delaware Valley—forty-five acres of Ingham Spring and Aquetong Lake.

As you travel across the backcountry roads of the New Hope environs, you will see rolling farmlands, primitive forests, and magnificent gardens. No matter what season, beautiful Bucks always has something to offer—a kaleidoscope of breathtaking flowers and scents in spring and summer; a blaze of brilliant colors in the fall; and a quiet drama of its own on frosty winter days.

Every Thursday, May through November, the people of New Hope can look forward to an abundant offering of fresh produce at our local Farmers' Market. As you wander from stall to stall, you can fill your eco-friendly shopping bag with an array of fresh vegetables and herbs, home-baked breads and muffins, organic poultry and eggs, sheep and goat's milk cheeses, healthy jams, jellies, and preserves, as well as, a variety of fresh-cut wild flowers. This weekly event supports the small farmers in our area and promotes an environmentally friendly lifestyle.

Living in New Hope gives one the opportunity to drive less and walk more. Many of us enjoy a brisk daily walk across the river bridge that connects us to our sister-town of Lambertville, New Jersey. You can cycle along the canal path, or bike along the back roads for miles and miles—either south to Washington Crossing Historic Park or north to Frenchtown, New Jersey. The area is filled with numerous trails for hiking and exploring. The beautiful landscape of this region makes these outdoor activities a most enjoyable and absorbing experience.

The Bucks County Audubon Society operates the Honey Hollow Environmental Center. Here is a place where young and old, families and school groups, locals and visitors alike can come to explore, appreciate, and learn more about wildlife and our natural environment. On this seven-hundred-acre property you can engage in such natural pleasures as . . . bird-watching, fishing, butterfly-raising, insect observation and (*croak*) frog-watching! This is a place that educates and demonstrates "green living" at its best.

You might have heard the saying, "To go out is really to go in." New Hope is a perfect retreat for those who are seeking a natural meditative setting. One can easily find a quiet spot for solitude, refreshment, and peace. With your eyes closed, it is easy to imagine the gentle people who first inhabited this beautiful area. The Lenni-Lenape Indians had such deep reverence for Mother Nature. They understood and practiced living in harmony with one another and with the land. The good people of New Hope have made an ongoing commitment to embrace that same sense of awe, respect, appreciation, and stewardship for the earth. We pride ourselves on living green.

Moving On

By Dorothea Hammond,
as told to Helen Rowe

When I first arrived in New Hope I was a sweet young thing, and, if I must say so myself, a rising star on the Great White Way. In the early 1940s, I had finished school, left my family home in Spring Lake, New Jersey, and had gone to New York City to pursue my dream of becoming a star on Broadway. While I took classes to polish my acting skills, I also enrolled in a dance academy and managed to do some part-time modeling (after all, an actor never knows when the next job will come along!). With persistence and determination, I began to get some lucky breaks into the world of theater. First, I started dancing in the choruses and then I took the plunge and began auditioning for performance roles. While I was working my way up to stardom, I happened to meet a brilliant, young, aspiring actor named Paul Hammond. We fell madly in love, married and settled into a little apartment on West Eighty-fifth Street.

I was thrilled to pieces when I landed a major supporting role in an original Broadway play titled *A Portrait in Black*. It was a classic suspense story—the plot included infidelity, murder, deceit, and blackmail. I had a featured role playing the part of a remote stepdaughter alongside of Claire Luce—the heroine. After opening night, I received an avalanche of favorable reviews from the critics. This was it. I felt like I was on my way. Tah-dah!

Then one day out of the blue my husband turned to me and said, "I've decided to make a major life change, dear." In short, he wanted to be an architect instead of an actor. I was floored. Then on top of that, Paul informed me that he wanted to move to Washington, D.C., another blow. *There goes my acting career,* I thought to myself. I felt torn apart by divided loyalties. I wanted to please my husband (whom I adored) and at the same time, I did not want to give up the theatrical success that I was just starting to experience in New York City. So what's a girl to do?

During this time of confusion and upheaval, I was offered a short reprieve. I got a call from the William Morris Agency asking if I'd like to be part of summer stock at the Bucks County Playhouse in New Hope, Pennsylvania. I talked it over with Paul and finally (with his approval), I made the decision to go.

In the late summer of 1949, I made my way to New Hope anxious to feel the thrill of getting back on stage again. The production I was hired for was a George Abbott comedy called *Three Men on a Horse*. It was a silly, screwball plot that revolved around a misfit greeting card poet who had a knack for picking winning horses and got himself mixed up with a gang of small-town gamblers. Think *Guys and Dolls* without the music! I played the part of Mabel, a ditsy, wise-cracking blonde with a thick Brooklyn accent who was one of the gangster's molls.

During my time in New Hope, I rented a room from two Quaker ladies who had a small home overlooking the river. Part of my daily routine was to lie in their backyard hammock, script in hand, practicing my lines out loud. "Come ovuh here, Oy-Win, cos ya know I like yooz allot." Did you get that? Come over here, Erwin, because you know I like you a lot. The play was a crazy, madcap, lighthearted farce. Nineteen characters were in the cast so there was a great deal of cavorting around the stage. It was filled with typical George Abbott comic devices— exaggerated action, split-second timing, doors opening and closing, et cetera. My most captivating moment on stage was a backwards, upside-down, fall into the lap of poor "Oy-Win." The guy didn't know what hit him. There I was, stretched out on his lap with my legs crossed sky-high in the air, with the curls from my blonde wig dangling onto the stage floor. The audience loved it.

When there was no action on the stage, there was still something else that captured the audience's attention. People loved looking at the famous "fire curtain" that had been painted by a New Hope artist named Charles Child. (Charlie was the twin brother of Julia Child's husband, Paul Child.) The huge, hand-painted curtain was filled with scenes depicting the town of New Hope and famous landmarks in the surrounding area. There was one little spot on the curtain that drew giggles from everyone . . . "See if you can find the nude sunbather!" It was like playing a game of "I Spy" while waiting for the show to begin.

Being part of summer stock theater at the Bucks County Playhouse not only fulfilled my desire to act, but it also gave me an opportunity to explore the beautiful countryside. Although I didn't have my own car, I would hitch a ride with someone else in the cast, and we would drive along the backcountry roads admiring the old stone houses, the rolling hills, the covered bridges, and the gorgeous farms. I remember that Moss Hart owned acres and acres of farmland somewhere along Aquetong Road. Other New York playwrights had also migrated to the New Hope area: George S. Kaufman, S.J. Perlman, and of course, Oscar Hammerstein II.

Walking along the streets of New Hope, you never knew whom you might run into. There always seemed to be many Broadway people milling around town. For a special treat, I would occasionally dine at the Playhouse Inn, a swanky restaurant right along the river's edge. It was in a cluster of buildings located on the left-hand side of the Playhouse. The place always seemed to be packed with stars and celebrities. I can still remember going there one evening and ordering a cup of cold tomato soup. It was divine . . . perfectly chilled, garnished with teeny slices of onion and dill and topped off with a dollop of crème fraiche. At the time, I was just starting to get interested in gourmet food and cooking. For years afterwards, I tried my best to replicate that wonderful chilled tomato soup, but I never found a recipe that came close.

I loved hanging out with the close-knit circle of fellow actors and actresses from the Playhouse. One night Jimmy Hammerstein (Oscar's son) invited all of us to a wild and zany party at his parent's farmyard estate. Someone recently showed me a brochure for a newly renovated bed and breakfast called "Highland Farms" that is located on the former Hammerstein property. Jimmy was just a kid then, maybe eighteen or nineteen-years-old, but even at that young age he was taken with the theater. He used to hang out in the wings of the Playhouse stage and loll around in the parking lot where a little refreshment stand was located. The cast and crew piled into a caravan of cars and headed out to the Hammerstein's estate near Doylestown. His parents were not home, in fact the house was locked up, but Jimmy opened up the barn for us, and we partied like crazy into the wee hours of the night.

That summer I spent in New Hope was like a shot in the arm for me. It filled me with hope that perhaps there was a way to continue my theatrical career outside of New York City. My husband and I moved to D.C. that fall. It was a huge adjustment for me at first, but eventually we moved from Tacoma Park, Maryland, to the historic and charming Georgetown area. In fact, I am still living in the same house that we bought over half a century ago. Once we moved here, I took some time off from the acting profession to focus on my private life. Eventually, I resumed my stage career and established a name and a place for myself in the Washington, D.C. theater world.

I still remember that day so many years ago, when I was sitting in my Upper West Side N.Y.C. apartment and my handsome, young husband announced to me that we were "moving on." I thought my acting career had reached a dead end. But New Hope showed me that it was only a bend in the road.

(Dorothea Hammond has lived in the Washington, D.C. area since the 1950s and is an iconic actress in the D.C. theater world.)

New Hope: Journey's End

By P. D. Cacek

I've been asked to answer a question that many others—friends, family, interviewers—have asked me for the past dozen years: What is the fascination people have with New Hope, Pennsylvania? Now, I could just say I don't know and make this the shortest written piece in history, but I do know. Or, at least, I think I do. But first, a little history—mine.

I first saw New Hope in 1997. I was attending a writing convention in Philadelphia when a friend offered to show me this "quaint little artsy-fartsy" town on the banks of the Delaware River. I figured the "artsy-fartsy" plug was more for my benefit than an actual indictment against the town itself. Since I was living in California (where the term undoubtedly began), my friend thought it would provide whatever impetus might be needed to get me to go.

In truth, I happen to like quaint little towns, "artsy-fartsy" or not, and the prospect of spending a few hours away from self-promoting agents, wall-to-wall book displays, inane panel discussions, and overpriced menu items seemed reason enough to head for the wilds of some place called Bucks County.

As I recall it was late afternoon on a hot June day and my friend decided to take the "scenic route" along River Road. It was the first time I can remember being completely surrounded by trees (and palm-lined boulevards do not count).

Every now and then my friend would point out a historic landmark—Washington's Crossing, Bowman's Hill, Odette's Restaurant, where news anchorwoman Jessica Savitch ate her last meal. Or I'd catch a glimpse of the river, but for the most part, it was like driving through a long green tunnel.

Then, more or less suddenly, the woods were behind us and a small sign welcoming us to the Borough of New Hope, Pennsylvania, flashed by. I could tell immediately that the little town was not *only* an artsy-fartsy town. It was crowded. In fact, I don't think I have ever seen so many people on a main street that did not have Disney characters walking on it, too. It was amazing, even for a jaded Californian.

Even more amazing—besides finding a parking spot next to the Aaron Burr Inn—was the feeling that came over me the moment I stepped out of the car. I had never even heard of New Hope and yet I had an immediate sense of belonging, as if I'd only been away for a while and had now come home. Every street seemed familiar.

Now this might have been odd anywhere else. And anywhere else, it would have been. But in New Hope it felt perfectly natural. I was home, somehow, and I had to write a book about it. This wasn't strange, since writers are always getting inspired—but my inspirations caught me while I was crossing Main Street and stopped me dead (directly in front on an oncoming truck).

Once my friend dragged me to the sidewalk and asked me what the Hell I thought I was doing, I told him about the book—beginning, middle and end, the character names, the plot twists (one of them about New Hope being haunted). And the fact that I had to write it in New Hope because that's where it was set. All this after maybe twenty minutes of seeing the town.

The problem was, that there was absolutely no way I could move to New Hope. At the time I was one of the expatriated Californians living in Colorado with a family to raise and obligations to meet. The idea that I would even be able to come back, let alone live in New Hope to write a book was ludicrous. Absolutely impossible. Couldn't happen in a million years. But I did.

A year later—and that's a story for another time—I was able to rent a basement apartment (with ghost) on New Street, discover New Hope is haunted—in fact the MOST haunted town in America, and finish the first draft of the novel. At the end of those seven months I left, thinking I would never return.

I was back the following year to help work on the documentary *"America's Most Haunted Town"* (directed by Rob Child) and left figuring, "This is it. Good-bye forever, New Hope." (Overly dramatic, I know, but I'm a writer.)

It took another couple of years, but I'm back in Pennsylvania, and even though I don't live in New Hope, I visit regularly. Because that's what old friends do—they visit.

Which brings us back to the original question: What IS the fascination people have with New Hope, Pennsylvania?

Finally, the answer. Also mine. (To be taken with a grain of salt, as needed.)

Now, this may be where that grain of salt comes in, but I think there's a tranquility here that invokes thoughts of journey's end and homecoming and whatever it is that comes to mind when we think of the word "home:" comfort, security, acceptance. Too metaphysical? Maybe, but you don't have to take my word for it. Look around and notice the faces of the people on the streets and in the shops—both tourists and residents alike. More often than not, there is a reflection of that tranquility in the way they speak or move or smile. They've come home, even if they live a hundred miles away.

Of course, if you ask them they might give you the name of their favorite restaurant or shop or bar or...fill in the blank, because, as I discovered when I started this piece, it really is hard to describe a feeling. But once you've felt it, it's even harder to leave it behind. So you keep coming back. Or you never leave, which is probably the reason New Hope IS the most haunted town in America. Home is where the stories start. And the stories in this book prove this. Welcome back.

Resurrection Park

By Daniel Brooks

The sun is setting as it does every day at a special, mostly uninhabited park, which I call Resurrection, just outside of New Hope near Aquetong Road and along the Delaware River. It has been my habit for over twelve years (the entire time I have lived in New Hope), to take a walk each Sunday in this slim, lush alcove, banked on one side by the river and the other by the historic towpath canal. I stand and watch the sun go down to the west, casting Bowman Tower in a shadow, and fall softly over the treetops until it finally disappears into the horizon.

I prefer to be there alone except for my dog as my companion. At Resurrection Park, she can be a real animal. She enjoys wading in the canal or taking a dunk in the Delaware. She smells the other animals that come out there at night to feed and drink—deer, rabbits, and sometimes an occasional beaver. She loves the wild smells of all the vegetation, whether it's in the growing or decaying stage. In the winter, the smells at Resurrection are crisp and clean. By sharp contrast, the air there is sultry and humid and our summer walk is slower, deliberately blissful, and aimless.

Spring is the great awakening at Resurrection Park because you can actually see, from week to week, the opening of buds, the regrowth of ground greenery and the return of the robins, blue jays, and cardinals. It is often spotlighted by sunny rays which, these days, stay warm longer and longer. My favorite season at the park is fall, since the blaze of color is packed into those few miles.

My collie dog, Dewey, has a coat of beige, brown, and tan that looks like camouflage wear during the autumn season at Resurrection Park because she blends into the colors of the fallen leaves and treetops. Her first trip as a pup was to this park, and she now knows every inch of it. She knows the path we travel each week, and every time we arrive at the park, she leaps from the car like an eager kid ready to explore this territory as if it were her first time.

When we get to the rudimentary railroad track ties, installed generations ago as steps leading to the river's edge, Dewey darts downward with deliberateness and glee. She may have just spent a week with me exploring the trash cans and public parks in New York City, but there is nothing that excites her more than the freedom written all over her face each week at Resurrection Park.

Every Sunday we spend some time in the cemetery at Resurrection, which houses twenty graves of "unknown soldiers" from the Revolutionary War. They are reminders to all that a group of brave rebels stood camp one frozen winter on their way to defend the right for freedom at the decisive Battle of Trenton, and some of them died for it on that very spot. There are wreaths on each grave, and a U.S. flag flies gloriously in all weather. Its base lists the original twelve colonies that broke with England to do their "own thing" and in doing so began a nation.

Generally it is deserted when we watch the sun go down from there, and Dewey loves to sprawl out on the great lawn and get scratched some while I talk to her and fuss with her coat, which has often picked up wood chips from the sticks she carries or burrs from the brambles we pass through along the way. Often I silently, in my head, work through my own problems of the moment while Dewey plays in the lawn.

Dewey and I feel lucky each week to be at Resurrection Park because ten years ago it was almost not possible for either of us. She was at a local puppy farm waiting to be adopted. The longer she remained at the farm the less likely she was to be adopted. As she started to get older, she was deemed less of a sale prospect. During this same time, I had a silent heart attack while teaching a step aerobics class in Lambertville and was diagnosed with a fatal genetic heart condition. I was told to make a decision regarding an immediate quadruple bypass surgery. Without it, the doctors said, my life would be cut unexpectedly short or, at best, I would have to give up things that I loved, like exercise and sports. A compromised life, a life less free.

I immediately went to the park to ponder the news and I thought about all the brave Revolutionists who have walked that same path, who made the decision to either fight for freedom, or retreat and live a compromised life. I made the decision right then and there to enter Lenox Hill Hospital the next day and fight it out.

At Lenox Hill they offered me suggestions on how to prepare mentally for the upcoming heart surgery. One of those suggestions involved imagery. They told me to choose a place that I could train my mind to go to when scared, frightened, or confused. It took me only a split second to choose Resurrection Park, the place where I had so often taken my troubles, anxieties, or worries and figuratively dumped them in the river. The place where all is calm and quiet, and everything is beautiful, and the energy of those brave soldiers and their fight for freedom inspires me each week.

I realized that park is the embodiment of the uniqueness of New Hope. It is the spirit of Native Americans who camped here during the birth of our civilization, the fortitude of those men who started a nation, the strength of the canal which brought industrial progress to a struggling economy, and the ever-flowing, watchful Delaware, that has seen it all go by as time passed.

As they wheeled me in the operating room, I said "good-bye" to my partner, Jason, and closed my eyes, drowning out all noise, focusing on seeing myself soon standing at "my" spot in Resurrection Park. It was the last image I remembered until I woke up a day later in recovery. That was in June 1999.

After a few days in the hospital, I was weak from having my whole body shut down from the operation. Imagine an old car that suddenly must be taken apart for repair—restarting the engine has to be done in stages, little by little. Although I could leave the hospital, my recovery would take months. I immediately requested a lift to New Hope, where I knew I could regain my strength much faster than in the city. I knew that I needed to be closer to Resurrection.

Once in New Hope, I started a daily process of getting up, getting dressed, and being driven to Resurrection Park. At first, I could handle walking only a few steps. Gradually a block, two blocks, a small circle, a larger circle. The day I made it down the railroad ties to the river, I was overjoyed!

During the weeks that followed, I went to the park–each day setting new goals for walking and charting each day's progress while peering at Bowman's Tower. I set the journey up that hill as the ultimate recovery goal. Instead of hurriedly passing by, constantly out of breath, I was now forced to go at a very slow pace. This enabled me to notice everything within the park—the changing plant life, the visiting bees and birds, the resident raccoons, the ebbs and flows of the water.

As I got stronger, I had a new appreciation for life and a definite new hope for my future. I felt that, though now a semi-invalid, if I could just make it to Bowman's Tower, my life would be mine again. I bargained with God, that, if that were to happen, I would do something meaningful for New Hope in return. Like the ancestors who strove to make life better, if I could just get well, I would do something, which would have an effect on the community of my rebirth. If "resurrected." I promised a payback.

After three weeks, I asked Jason to join me, and he and I triumphantly made it to Bowman's Tower and back. What was once the simplest walk had now been my monumental climb to recovery. That week, Jason surprised me with that sweet little puppy that had been waiting patiently on the farm, and said, "Now you will have someone to walk with you at the park." I could not wait to show Dewey the ropes of Resurrection, where we could both start our new lives together. I also started thinking about how to keep my recovery promises.

That same year I had an opportunity to purchase a dilapidated one-hundred-and-seventy-year-old farmhouse in New Hope and save it from a wrecker's ball. For six months, I worked in New York during the week and worked weekends on the property. By Memorial Day, 2000, I realized a dream of my father's (also a victim of heart disease) to have a family-inn business. I opened that property as the Wishing Well Guesthouse, named in gratitude for my becoming well.

Three years later, in 2003, I went before New Hope Borough Council and asked if I could initiate a gay and lesbian pride festival in town. That was realizing yet another dream . . . to bring recognition and honor to a town known for its diversity and nonconformists. It was the beginning of New Hope Celebrates, which is now a nonprofit marketing organization holding nationally advertised events, among them the annual gay pride festival and parade.

Later I took the reins of a town treasure, the *New Hope Gazette,* and had the opportunity and honor to be its editor for a wonderful year. In all three instances, I was able to fulfill promises made for life renewed at Resurrection Park.

Tonight my Dewey, saved from an undecided future a decade ago, and I, saved from near death at the same time, are here at Resurrection Park, and as always, we are watching the sun go down. I have been asked to write a story about my experience and attachments to New Hope and just now, petting Dewey, I realize that right here, in this park, is my story. I could have—genetically, should have—lost my life in New Hope ten years ago, but I was given a second chance...an opportunity for resurrection, and the park has seen me through it.

That is what New Hope has done for me, and for many, many others. For centuries it has given folks a second chance, another look, a point of view or reference, a bucolic, verdant home where all of us feel that anything can happen if we set our minds to it. Like my experience at Resurrection Park, New Hope provides the climate, environment, and opportunity for all, but it is up to us to take the action and do the resurrecting.

Dewey, who is lying vigilantly by my side here in the park while keeping watch on a pack of approaching white-tailed deer, agrees with me wholeheartedly.

It Has a Way of Finding You

By Laura Schrock

FADE UP:

I guess the creative drive kicked in somewhere back in high school. I was running for VP of Student Council. An ad campaign was out then for Lucky Strike cigarettes (one of the very few vices I've managed to dodge). It read: LSMFT: *Lucky Strike Means Fine Tobacco.* So my campaign was LSMFT: *Laura Schrock Means Future Triumphs*! (I took it upon myself to add the exclamation point.) And hey, I won! Far out! I was a creative advertising genius! Kind of…That propelled me to college where I stumbled upon acting, directing, and writing—all those great courses that scare the hell out of parents. Oh, and I played lead guitar in an all-girl rock band too. Yeah, the folks were looking at the college tuition, looking at me, and saying, "This is all great, but what are you going to fall back on?" At that point, it wasn't about falling. It was about Women's Lib, Free Love, and when is the next Beatles album coming out? You know, STUFF THAT REALLY MATTERED! *Ahhh, the past…*

SMASH CUT TO: New York City.

After college, a mad, wild, hectic career set in: I was living in N.Y.C. and doing Live TV. That's when I first learned to grind my teeth. Deadlines, celebs with ultimatums, high rents, late nights, romantic crushes, and big stress: *Ahhh, youth…* N.Y.C. was the very first love of my life. It captured my heart before anything and anyone. While living there, a few geographical and social things became clear: I did not want to trek to those Hamptons. I did like Connecticut in the fall. And the weekend jaunts to New Hope, Pennsylvania? Hands down, those were the weekends that soothed my urban soul. And I never, ever forgot that. Somehow, among all the craziness and events that have seeped into my life since my first visit to New Hope back in 1981, I have managed to hold onto the magic of this Bucks County gem.

So, after having put twenty-two years into a TV career in Los Angeles, I decided to follow my instincts and return East. That was back in 2006. Since then, I can tell you point-blank, moving to this great town was one of the best life decisions I ever made. My creative juices have never been stronger. It is hard not to be inspired when you are surrounded by four seasons of ongoing beauty and special people. I have taken creative risks here that I would never have done anywhere else. Could I have done *It's Todd's Show*—my wacky web show with talking dogs and a cast of zanies anywhere other than "live and let live, anything goes" New Hope? Don't think so. Actually, let me revise that: NO!

New Hope people are special. They carry a sense of trust, positivity, and calm that resonates—and it fills the soul. Maybe it's because it is so darn gorgeous here, the beauty seems to seep into everyone's persona culminating in all these wonderful folks that make the area so special. I knew I'd hit the jackpot when, after having a dinner party, a *handwritten* thank you note showed up in the mail. It might as well have been a gold brick. Then, a few weeks later, the meal was reciprocated. Another time, after a snowstorm, a new friend around the corner just showed up and started plowing the driveway. Yep. People here take the time to care. They relish the moment. They give of their time. They respect the past. And they know how to have fun. *That's* for sure.

I cannot tell you how many times I've walked Bridge and Main Streets, looked at the visitors on a Sunday afternoon, and said to myself: "I'm not visiting! I get to live here!" (This is usually followed by an ice cream cone or mojito depending on my mood.) Thanks for embracing *me*, New Hope—'cause I'm hugging you back with everything I've got!

FADE OUT

The Gift That Keeps On Giving

By Curt Plott

I am married to the Queen of Everything. Our home in Washington, D.C. is known as the "House of Stuff." No kidding. I'm telling you this so you will know what a challenge it is for me every time a special holiday rolls around and I rack my brain to think of a gift for my lovely wife. The pressure is on at least three times a year. Let's see—there is a November birthday, followed by Christmas. Then comes Valentine's Day, which is always a "double-whammy" because it is also our Anniversary.

You get the picture. It is impossible to buy anything for my wife. After twenty years of marriage, I have exhausted almost every idea. I have given her jewelry, clothes, shoes, original artwork, opera tickets, gift certificates, personalized license plates—just to name a few. (Take note, guys, there's nothing "practical" on that list.) Sometimes, in desperation, I turn to Lynda and say, "Okay, just tell me what you want." To which she usually replies, "A surprise," or "Just get me something frivolous." Not much help. But, many years ago, I did get a great clue from her. "If you want to get me something really special," she said, "how about taking me to New Hope for a weekend rendezvous?"

My wife grew up in the Bucks County area. Her parents lived there for over forty-five years. My mother-in-law was the one-and-only Adi-Kent Thomas Jeffrey who started the New Hope ghost tours many years ago. Even though my wife has been a D.C. resident ever since she graduated from George Washington University (and I'm not telling you how many years ago that was), I know she has never lost her attachment to New Hope. She always speaks of New Hope as her favorite place in the world. She still refers to it as her "Home, Sweet Home."

A trip to New Hope. That's what my wife asked for and that's what she got. I let her make all the arrangements. She picked out the place to stay, made all of the restaurant reservations, and lined-up the social activities with some of her old friends. We traveled there in the fall for her birthday, and the autumn foliage was unbelievable. I can still remember driving those last few miles along the narrow strip of River Road as we started heading into town. "God, this is beautiful," is all I could say. We drove to the Stockton Inn for her birthday dinner. What a rustic and charming place. We sat in the room where the walls are covered with hand-painted murals. As we sipped champagne at our fireside table, I thought to myself, "This is as good as it gets."

That trip marked my first real visit to New Hope. And, okay, I'll admit it. I was hooked. These days my wife and I are both retired so we return to New Hope as much as we like and as often as we can.

We have taken other family members as well as many good friends along with us on some of these trips. To this day, Lucy and Alice (our two granddaughters) still talk about New Hope. They have never forgotten their ride on the old-fashioned steam locomotive, their first spin on a merry-go-round at Giggleberry Fair, and sitting in the front row of the Bucks County Playhouse watching the show *Bye Bye Birdie*. Of course, the highlight of the trip for the girls was a shopping spree at Love Saves the Day. They blew their whole allowance on buying some fake dog poop, which they then proceeded to "hide" in my shoes. Ask my granddaughters about New Hope and most likely you'll get a one-word answer, "Cool."

Last year, my wife was one of the exhibitors at the New Hope Arts and Crafts Festival. This annual event has been going on for the past fifteen years—rain or shine, I might add. All I can say is 2008 was definitely a year to remember. Non-stop torrential rain for the entire weekend. Normally our trips to New Hope consist of nothing but leisure and pleasure, however this time we were there to work. A caravan of friends followed us from D.C. helping to haul along all of Lynda's "stuff." It was raining cats and dogs, but we got the booth set up and resurrected when it collapsed, and in spite of the monsoon-like weather, we had a terrific time. We laughed, we joked, we teased my wife unmercifully, and after closing down shop each night we recovered at Zoubi's Bar by drinking some of Ricky's outrageous mango martinis.

It was a memorable weekend. And, hey, my wife ended up getting the last laugh of all—she actually made a profit. What we learned is that the New Hope Arts and Crafts Festival has a loyal following no matter what Mother Nature decides to do.

I never thought that I would love any place as much as Southern California. That's where I grew up, went to college, and where I also lived and worked for many years. Laguna Beach (where my son lives) is still my idea of heaven. But, I have been an East Coast guy now for several decades and, thanks to my wife, I've discovered that New Hope gives me a similar sense of happiness. It's not the same, but there is an equivalent feeling of peace, tranquility, and contentment.

What began as a present for my wife has now become an ongoing "gift" to us both. I can honestly say I love New Hope as much as she does. It is not a long drive from D.C. We usually make it in about three hours as we zoom through those tollbooths in the E-ZPass lane and once we are there, I can settle back and start to unwind. We each have our own routines. Lynda would not miss getting up at 6 AM on a Tuesday morning to hit Rice's Market no matter what. Yeah, that's right . . . she is out there buying more "stuff" while I like to make Farley's my first stop. Now that's a bookshop that is completely crazy and chaotic, and I love it. Where else can you be looking over a stack of best sellers and find yourself getting nudged by a big, yellow cat? Only in New Hope could a stray feline wander through a shopkeeper's door and end up finding a permanent home among rows and rows of books. Let's hear it for "Butter"!

Like most couples, we carve out enough time each day to do our own thing. She shops and I read, but what we enjoy most is being together. New Hope is a fabulous place for romantic dinners and late-night drinks. The first time Lynda took me to the Phillips Mill Inn I felt like I had been transported to the Cotswolds in England. I have never found another restaurant that offers such a good deal . . . a charming atmosphere, great gourmet food, the most exuberant waitress I've ever met (that would be you, Ingrid) and to top it all off, you can bring your own wine. What's not to like?

The two of us love hanging out at Tuscany at the Towpath House. Paul Licitra always rolls out the red carpet for us. We normally don't eat many sweets, but who can resist Paul's homemade tiramisu? We never fail to stop by and see Andre at Zoubi Bar and Restaurant. I think Andre has a crush on my wife. He always gives us the best table in the house (in the little nook that overhangs the street) and after dinner, he will sometimes shuffle over to us with a complimentary dessert. "Theez ez my own bread pudding. Eeet's better than sex," he says. No matter how many times we have heard those lines, we still laugh our heads off.

We love popping in to Marsha Brown's for a late night drink at the bar. We've also experienced a memorable night at Havana when one of our local friends dragged us down there on a Monday evening for karaoke with Rockin' Ron. Even after two martinis, folks, I did not get up to sing. The tavern room at the Logan Inn is another one of our favorite nightspots. As we sip our wine near the fireside, Lynda will often regale me with one of her mother's spooky stories about that place.

In conclusion, I have to say the one thing that makes our many sojourns to New Hope especially enjoyable is the fact that we have now established the most wonderful home away from home. We used to make the rounds from one bed and breakfast to another. We loved them all for different reasons, and it was a lot of fun to try new places, but once Lynda found "Porches" she announced to me, "This is it." When we booked a room in the gatekeeper's cottage and Lynda discovered that huge antique porcelain soaking tub, she poured in the bubble bath, settled in for hours of relaxation and said to me, "If this isn't heaven, then I don't want to go there." The warm welcome we always receive from John and Chrissie and Spencer Davis (the house cat otherwise known as "Le Chat Lunatic") makes us feel like we're not just guests at the inn—we're "family."

Certainly, we have cut back on our family expenses during these economic hard times. My wife, who loves to celebrate every holiday, has tried to steer our gift giving into a new direction. Some of her suggestions include books (I can go for that one), something homemade (easy for her, tough for me), writing each other letters of appreciation (fine, I can do that), and planning a romantic "staycation" at home (fits the budget—that's for sure). No matter what happens on Wall Street, however, I can guarantee you there is one "Get-Away" vacation spot that will always remain at the top of our list—and that's New Hope,

Pennsylvania. There is no place on the East Coast we would both rather be. What started out as a birthday gift to my wife years ago is now our traditional "playcation" and the ultimate rendezvous for us both. The best way to put it is simply this: New Hope is the gift that just keeps on giving.

(Curt Plott, an international traveler and resident of Washington, D.C., is a former CEO of a non-profit association.)

Nakashima, Knowledge, and New Hope

By Stephen A. Glassman

In 1961, when I was ten years old, my parents took us on a day trip to New Hope, Pennsylvania, to visit George Nakashima's furniture studio on Aquetong Road. It took nearly four hours to drive to his sanctuary in the woods from our home in Baltimore, Maryland. I-95, which had just been started two years before, was incomplete and we constantly had to get on and off the interstate highway system. My sister and I played "Hangman" and "Beaver" along the way, identifying license plates from as many different states as we could find on the roads that wove through Maryland, Delaware, and Pennsylvania.

When we arrived at the great designer's studio, I immediately sensed that this was going to be a very special day for all of us. After parking our Oldsmobile Vista Cruiser station wagon in the gravel parking area, we were invited into a small building and asked to sign a guest book, which was closely guarded by Mrs. Nakashima. I remember noticing that she was even smaller than my mother who was only five feet tall. We waited for a few minutes on beautiful wooden benches with wide curving seats and spindle backs until a small Japanese man entered the room and asked us to walk with him to another building on the property. We moved quietly down a path, where each flagstone was artfully placed amid a bed of moss, guiding us downhill toward a vaulted-roof structure that was entered by crossing a small bridge onto a serene wooden deck overlooking a beautifully landscaped valley below.

Before entering this building, we were asked to remove our shoes and to replace them with soft slippers, none meant for the feet of young children. I came to realize that this was a place for adults and that we were very lucky to be included in this adventure with our parents. I did not know who this famous furniture maker was and had never met anyone of Japanese descent in person before. I only knew that we were there to buy dining room furniture and a bench for our foyer, like the one we had rested on in the waiting pavilion. I did not realize that we would only order the furniture that day and then wait for more than a year and a half for it to arrive.

George Nakashima was extremely patient with my need to try out every piece of furniture in the showroom gallery before sitting down with us to sketch out our new table, chairs, buffet, and hall bench on a piece of handmade Japanese paper with frayed edges. I was mesmerized throughout the entire experience and charmed by this man who seemed both old and full of energy at the same time.

Compared with my parents, who were then in their thirties, Mr. Nakashima seemed as old as my grandparents. He spoke slowly and quietly, his words carefully chosen and spare. Then he put his arm around my shoulder and asked me if I wanted to go down to the basement below the studio to help him pick out the pieces of wood for our dining room table. I looked at my parents for permission and they easily gave their approval for George Nakashima and his young apprentice to select the wood slabs for this important piece of furniture for our home in the suburbs of Baltimore.

I left the Nakashima compound that day feeling both important and proud of my role in choosing the table at which Shabbat dinners and Passover Seders would be served for the next forty-five years. I sensed even at the age of ten that this place was somehow magical and that what we had accomplished together as a family would change our lives in a way that I could not quite comprehend. Years later, after I had graduated from the Yale School of Architecture and purchased my first home in Baltimore, I returned to George Nakashima's studio and ordered a dining table for myself. This time the drive only took two and a half hours because the highway system was completed (except for the stretch on either side of the Philadelphia International Airport).

I sat at the very same desk in his showroom and watched the great master sketch the lines of my own dining room table with butterfly joints and a conoid base. I went down the stairs with him to select the Persian walnut slabs out of which this massive ten-foot-long table would be constructed. Once again, Mr. Nakashima, older and a bit shorter than he had been fifteen years earlier, put his arm around my shoulder. He reminded me of the day he had entertained an inquisitive, talkative, whirlwind of boy energy in his studio while he sketched out a dining room table for a doctor and his wife from Baltimore, who had arrived with their two children in tow to explore a world as far away from their own as Japan was from the United States.

Five years later I purchased a weekend home with my then-partner, a few miles north of New Hope on the Delaware River. I returned to New Hope, as a child comes back to its mother, feeling a sense of comfort and belonging that no other place could offer. It was partly because it was a place where it was so easy to be gay. But in a more profound sense, it was because George Nakashima had made this picturesque hamlet on the Delaware River a place of memory, artistry, and serenity for me that could never be matched in its singular beauty anywhere else on this earth.

(Stephen A. Glassman is chairperson of the Pennsylvania Human Relations Commission and vice chairperson of the Governor's Cabinet on Disability Rights.)

Afterword

Assembling, editing, and reading the submitted works by all the authors has been a real education for me, and I hope you, the readers, have been as equally enlightened and entertained. New Hope is a special place; there can be little doubt. And I can say that I really hadn't thought about my own "coming to New Hope" story until recently.

Surprisingly there is a little of my own story in several of our authors' stories. My first trip was with my sister who had received her driver's license and commandeered the car, and my mother. We shopped; I bought a hand-tooled, leather belt, and we ate at one of the New Hope restaurants. Several years later, when I became a student at Trenton State College (now The College of New Jersey), I knew New Hope to be one of the "cool" places to hangout. Later still, it was the bars and dance clubs. Bringing a friend's six-year-old daughter to the New Hope-Ivyland Santa Express made the list too. There was always a New Hope siren call, bringing me back to New Hope.

Then along came Geri Delevich. Her belief and love of her hometown of New Hope became contagious. Her wish to spread the goodness and kindness of people and the essence of what she has found in New Hope became the foundation of Up River Productions. This book, these stories, is the catalyst to share the message, her message.

So it just goes to show, we all have a New Hope story. What will yours be?

Marilyn Cichowski

About the Editors

Geri Delevich is happy to call New Hope, Pennsylvania, home for more than thirty-five years. She is an elected official on the New Hope Borough Council, serving her twelfth year. As an elementary school teacher for thirty-three years, Geri saw the value in respect for each student and their individual talents and perspectives. Believing in respect and equality for all, Geri initiated the landmark non-discrimination ordinance supporting equality for the lesbian, gay, bisexual, and transgender community in the borough of New Hope. For her work in this area, she accepted the Human Rights Campaign Equality Award on behalf of the borough of New Hope. Geri was also honored for her many community achievements by the Lambertville, New Jersey-New Hope, Pennsylvania International Rotary Club. Geri was one of the founders of the volunteer organization HOPE—Helping Other People Everyday, produced a documentary honoring senior members of New Hope, and helped to initiate the borough's outdoor sculpture program. She hopes the Embraceable You project will encourage an environment of understanding and a celebration of our diversity.

Marilyn Cichowski has lived in the area since attending and graduating from The College of New Jersey. She holds a master of arts degree from Rutgers University. Marilyn spent her career serving the state of New Jersey as an investigator and retired from the Commission of Investigation as a Senior Special Agent. She has been a long time believer of an individual's quest for authenticity and the interdependent web of all existence—values central to being a member of Unitarian Universalism. She is a corporate officer of Up River Productions, Inc.

Up River Productions, Inc. was created and incorporated in the state of Pennsylvania in 2007. Up River Productions, Inc. is recognized by the Internal Revenue Service as a 501(c) (3) charitable organization. Its mission is to advance and promote equality, non-violence, non-discrimination, anti-racism, diversity, and inclusion. All proceeds of the sale of this book will further the mission of Up River Productions, Inc. To learn more about The Embraceable You project, including a documentary and compilation CD, visit the website: www. UpRiverProductions.com.

Up River Productions, Inc.
P.O. Box 484
New Hope, PA 18938

CPSIA information can be obtained
at www.ICGtesting.com
Printed in the USA
FSOW04n0953271217
42794FS